THE MIRACLE BOOK

(God made Miracles for You—and YOU for Miracles)

D1108843

By Oral Roberts

Sequel to MIRACLE OF SEED-FAITH

FIRST PUBLISHED EDITION

FIRST PRINTING, 200,000—MARCH 1973
SECOND PRINTING, 100,000—APRIL 1973
THIRD PRINTING, 100,000—MAY 1973
FOURTH PRINTING, 200,000—MAY 1973
FIFTH PRINTING, 100,000—JUNE 1973
SIXTH PRINTING, 100,000—JULY 1973
SEVENTH PRINTING, 200,000—JULY 1973

THE

SECRET

OF

LIFE

IS

IN

EXPECTING

MIRACLES!

1 THE MOST IMPORTANT THING IN YOUR LIFE IS A MIRACLE . . . ESPECIALLY WHEN YOU NEED ONE

FOR MORE THAN 25 YEARS I have been an instrument of God's miracle power. Now, more than ever, I am ministering to people whose only hope to LIFE is in miracles.

Friend, Jesus Christ HIMSELF is the greatest of all miracles—the continuing living miracle. The miracles I am talking about for you are *living* and *existing* in the MAN . . . the Man Christ Jesus.

A miracle is not an accident. It doesn't happen by doing nothing. You don't get it for nothing. A miracle comes through faith . . . faith in God, faith in yourself, faith that the seed you put in will be multiplied back to you. This is why, in 1969, I wrote the book, MIRACLE OF SEED-FAITH. More than one million families wrote for it. It literally exploded in them, showing them the possibility of using their faith in a definite scriptural way and bringing miracles right into their everyday lives. Every day many other people hear about MIRACLE OF SEED-FAITH, write for it, and start their own demonstration of God's abundance with the 3 MIRACLE KEYS . . .

Key No. 1: God is the Source of your Total Supply . . . (Philippians 4:19).

Key No. 2: Seeding for your Miracle . . . (Luke 6:38).

Key No. 3: Expect a Miracle . . . (Mark 11:24).

5

And thousands of these dear people have gone from:
sickness to health ...
worry to faith ...
bitterness to love ...
a mountain of bills to financial security ...
a problem-centered marriage to a Christ-centered one ...
self-doubt to a deep faith that God is in control of their lives ...
Christ meaning little or nothing to a vital, personal Christian witness!
and from a worry-filled life to God's gift of the Holy Spirit and power.

I tell you it is exciting to read their letters! Let me just share a few sentences from some of these letters with you:

"God healed me--it's a miracle!!!"

"I received a miracle in my marriage..."

"Jesus saved my son who was on drugs...now he's turned on to Christ..."

"I had not been able to pay my bills...then I got hold of Miracle of Seed-Faith...it changed my thinking. Now, thank God, I can pay my bills, with something left over..."

"No wonder I didn't see miracles in my life--I never gave of myself or my possessions. Brother Roberts, you showed me how to use my faith. Now I feel like a new person..."

"I WAS ON THE VERGE OF BANKRUPTCY when I got hold of Miracle of Seed-Faith...I read it over and over until it became a part of me. I started Seed-Faith living and am finding that day-by-day it works..."

6

"My adult Sunday school class in the United Methodist Church has been studying your book, Miracle of Seed-Faith. Your statement, 'Expect a Miracle,' has generated a revival in our church!"

"Since we started practicing the 3 KEYS of Seed-Faith living, life has been in stereo and full color!"

"OUR FAMILY WAS IN TROUBLE...we couldn't relate to each other. My husband and I lost touch with our children...through your telecast we came to know God in a more personal way. We began studying Miracle of Seed-Faith and putting the 3 KEYS to work in our lives. Now God is working--it isn't magic or easy, but He is working and He is working miracles. Now we are in a position to help others..."

"May the Lord bless you for all the encouragement and for your wonderful monthly letters. They are full of inspiration. Through your letters, literature, and Abundant Life magazine I learned about the baptism with the Holy Spirit. Now I have received the fullness of the Holy Spirit, and the feeling is just wonderful."

There are hundreds more and they pour across my desk daily. And how great it is to share in their victories.

On the other hand, in the same mail have been letters saying:

"I can't understand Seed-Faith ..."

"I'm trying to make the 3 KEYS of Seed-Faith work, but it isn't working—why?"

"Write another book, Brother Roberts; you haven't told us enough ..."

While I get a tremendous thrill from the testimonies of

Seed-Faith working miracles in so many people's lives; on the other hand, I am extremely anxious to have those who apparently have not grasped it yet, to tell me like it is. Then I can give them further help. Perhaps this is one reason this book, THE MIRACLE BOOK, has been welling up in me for months. It is my response to those who want to go deeper into Seed-Faith, and to answer others' requests for more information.

I am absolutely convinced that the 3 KEYS of Seed-Faith are the KEY teachings of the work and life of our Savior Jesus Christ, for the day-to-day living you must do on this earth. The 3 KEYS do not save your soul. Your faith in the living Christ and in His death and resurrection, saves you.

The 3 KEYS actually bring you into discipleship OR INTO FOLLOWING JESUS IN THE NOW . . . IN THE NOW-MOMENT OF WHAT YOU FACE IN LIFE . . . here on this earth—*BEFORE* YOU GET TO HEAVEN. The 3 KEYS are applicable to every need you have. They will work—fantastically—if you will work them. But before Seed-Faith can mean *anything* to you, you must TURN ON TO JESUS—AND TO MIRACLES.

OPEN YOUR MIND TO A NEW CONCEPT OF GOD—GOD, WHO IS THE SOURCE OF YOUR TOTAL SUPPLY!

OPEN YOUR MIND TO A NEW KIND OF GIVING—I CALL THIS SEEDING FOR YOUR MIRACLE BY GIVING FIRST!

OPEN YOUR MIND TO GOD'S ETERNAL LAW THAT WHAT YOU GIVE IS A SEED YOU PLANT. AND FROM THE SEEDS OF FAITH YOU SOW YOU CAN EXPECT MANY MIRACLES!

Learn from my experience and others' how to put your faith to work, how to look at your needs—not with horror and disgust, but as *the meeting place between you and Jesus*. How to see Jesus at the point of a need you have. How to see Him sitting where you sit, and feeling what you feel. How to become part of the answer rather than part of the problem.

Believe me, you already have this kind of faith. The Bible says you have it. "For God hath dealt [given] to every man the measure of faith" (Romans 12:3). The very act of reading this book and of wanting a miracle shows you that you have this God-given measure of faith . . . and you have it now. And I say with all my heart—*Never doubt the power of your own faith! Never! Never!*

I wish I could claim credit for everything in this book, but I can't. There were FLASHES of inspiration within my inner man that I felt as definitely as I breathe. There were moments of POWER flowing through me like liquid fire. THERE WERE TIMES I FELT MY SOUL WAS ON FIRE AND I COULDN'T STAND STILL. In other words, I was conscious God was adding words to mine, thoughts to mine, inspiration to mine,

and remember . . .

I LIVE WITH PEOPLE!

I didn't write this book closed off from people. I was not sitting in a comfortable chair, removed from the common needs and hurts of people as they face life in the NOW. I LIVED this book in the arena of human need and hopelessness. I was with people like yourself, hearing them talk, feeling their spirit, experiencing what they faced. I laughed with them, cried with them, believed with them when it was hard. And I felt Jesus; OH! I felt Him!

I KNOW THE MAN . . . JESUS CHRIST OF NAZARETH

I know Him better than I know any man. Better than I

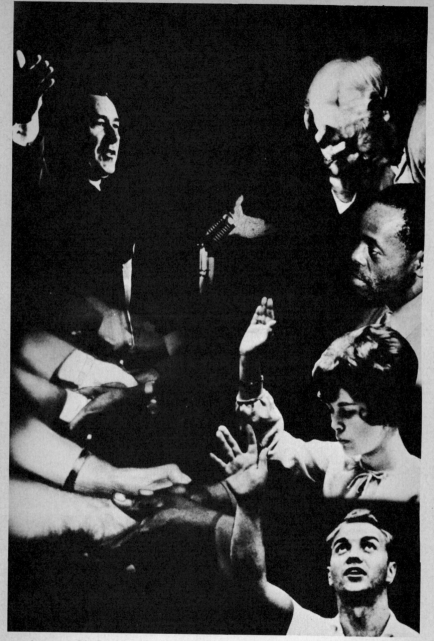

I wrote this book in the arena of human needs and hopelessness . . .

know my wife or children or my closest friends.

I walk with Him, talk with Him, feel Him, love Him, and trust Him.

He talks with me and walks with me.
He knows my strengths and weaknesses.
When I'm up, when I'm down,
He is CONSTANT in my life.
I can depend on Him.
He has never let me down.
And He never will. Not here . . .
not now . . .
not ever.

As you read this book I expect you to feel the Spirit of God going through you from time to time. I expect flashes of intuition, inspiration, and divine knowledge to come to you. I expect you to find yourself TURNING TO JESUS, AND THEN . . .

SEEDING FOR MIRACLES IN YOUR LIFE!
God bless you and prosper you—and He will!

I CHALLENGE YOU TO READ THIS WHOLE BOOK IN ONE WEEK . . . THEN READ SOME PART OF IT EVERY DAY. MARK PASSAGES THAT YOU FIND ESPECIALLY HELPFUL. KEEP IT ALONGSIDE YOUR BIBLE. READ ALL THE SCRIPTURAL REFERENCES I'VE INDICATED. WRITE ME OFTEN. I ENJOY LETTERS THAT MY FRIENDS WRITE ME. REMEMBER, GOD LOVES YOU; HE WANTS TO GIVE YOU MANY MIRACLES.

This is my brother Vaden and me (I'm on the right). If God could raise me up from poverty, from stammering and stuttering, and then heal me of tuberculosis—He can perform miracles for anybody.

2 MIRACLES—THE LAST FRONTIER YOU MUST CROSS— AND YOU CAN

WHAT I AM ABOUT TO TELL you in Chapter 2 is THE KEY to understanding all I am trying to teach you in this entire book. Therefore, I urge you to pay close attention to it. Study it carefully. It represents much of what the Holy Spirit has revealed to me about miracles since I wrote MIRACLE OF SEED-FAITH 3 years ago. Again, I urge you to study it prayerfully and carefully.

I remember in my life when I knew so little about miracles I wouldn't have recognized one if I had met it in the middle of the road. God was a blurrr in my mind. As the fellow said, who had been down so long, "Getting up hadn't crossed my mind."

I know there are people today who say they don't believe in miracles. They don't feel the need of miracles. Well, as I said to a group in a talk recently, it's been my experience that nobody believes in miracles until he needs one. It's when you need one that you start thinking about it.

The key is the need . . . and feeling the need. That's because, intuitively, we feel something about miracles. Miracles settle the issue. Miracles get the job done.

The fact is, there is a God-implanted urge in every human being for miracles. God made you for miracles, and He made miracles for you. Therefore—

THE VERY SECRET OF LIFE IS IN EXPECTING MIRACLES. MIRACLES—THE LAST FRONTIER YOU MUST CROSS —AND YOU CAN.

You can because of Jesus, who is both Son of God and SON OF MAN. I want to talk to you about this for a little while. This is very important to you.

I talked with a man recently whose marriage was breaking up just at the time when they thought they had enough material goods to have it made. But he confessed that somewhere he and his wife had somehow missed what it takes to have a happy life. I looked at him, then at her. They looked good. Nice clothes. A fine name and standing in the community. But down inside, something was eating away their hearts.

Well, to me, JESUS is the answer to any need, especially when you apply the 3 KEYS. And I knew, in spite of what appeared to be a marriage that was going to break up forever, they could have a miracle through God. And I told them so.

A puzzled look came over the man's face. He said, "Oral, I don't want to offend you, but what has this guy Jesus got to do with it?"

I said, "Do you admit you need a miracle?"

He said, "Yes, I admit that."

"And if you got it, everything would be all right again?"

"Yes. I believe it would."

I said, "Then you've got to start with THE MAN HIMSELF, the One who made you for miracles and made miracles for you. Miracles for life in the NOW start in Him— THE MAN JESUS!"

He said, "I just don't understand this. What has Jesus got to do with me and my problem?"

14

Perhaps you, too, are asking about Jesus or about miracles, and you're not getting answers either. I understand how you feel for, just like this man, I went through the same thing at a certain time in my life—and still do sometimes.

I talked with this couple at length and was able to help them. And I believe what I said to them will help you. Here, in essence, is what I told them, and what I want to share with you ABOUT THE MAN JESUS, concerning you and your need. It is a piece of information so important that you've GOT to know it. As you study it you'll be able to shorten your learning experience and come into a deeper KNOWLEDGE OF JESUS, and learn how He will meet your needs down here on the level where you live. This is why I say it's so *tremendously important to you* . . . HERE IT IS . . .

When the time came in God's dealing with men that He couldn't get through to us any other way, He performed the most unusual miracle of all—

Not by giving the Ten Commandments by a miracle, as He did to Moses and the children of Israel at Mount Sinai . . .

Nor by the miracle of establishing them as a special nation with strict laws and dietary rules . . .

Nor by the miracle of raising up prophets to call them back to repentance and righteousness.

GOD PERFORMED THE GREATEST MIRACLE OF ALL BY COMING DOWN TO EARTH AND BECOMING A MAN, A HUMAN BEING. In what we call the INCARNATION God became flesh, restoring direct communication between man and himself. But more than that, as man He humanly experienced what all humans go through. Now this is a divine mystery and can only be comprehended by faith.

Here I am in ORU's Mabee Center teaching on "The Holy Spirit In The Now!" More than 1,400 are enrolled in this evening class (2 hours once a week) from both ORU's academic students and adults from the greater Tulsa area, some driving 200 miles round trip for each session.

The Son of God was ALSO Son of man. He sat where you sit and feels what you feel. He lived on earth like you do—therefore He is the only one qualified to lift you up into salvation, into making you a whole person, and into meeting ALL your needs.

Now follow me very closely. There were three things that had to happen for God to become man:

1. Jesus' entry to earth and becoming man in physical,

16

visible form and subject to our limitations, including death.

2. His return to heaven after 33 years on this earth where He had taken upon himself our sins, diseases, fears, oppressions of the devil, loneliness, frustrations, loss, and death itself.

3. His reentry to earth through the Holy Spirit. Not in His former physical, visible form—limited to time and space and death—but in His spiritual, invisible form—His glorified form in which He becomes to us the full, unlimited Christ, and INDWELLING MEN BY HIS SPIRIT, THE HOLY SPIRIT—He would bring a baptism IN the Holy Spirit (Acts 1:5) with "power from on high," working through us by divine grace and gifts of the Holy Spirit so that we would have immediate and continuous ACCESS to the unlimited resources of God for our LIMITATIONS.

(Please reread these three important events before you go further in the book.)

Now, let's talk about His ENTRY to earth. This was by a miraculous birth—the Holy Spirit coming upon the young virgin Mary, and conceiving in her God's holy Son (Matthew 1:20). Later on Jesus grew to manhood and, being about 30, He himself was "filled with the Holy Spirit." The Bible says the Spirit came upon Him in the bodily form of a dove (Mark 1:10). And from that moment He was led/driven by the Spirit in conflict with the devil (Mark 1:12, 13; Luke 4:1). C-O-N-F-L-I-C-T. He faced the devil exactly as you do, the same kinds of temptation, everything; nothing was left out that strikes at you today.

But because Jesus had the infilling of the Holy Spirit He was able to live in the power of the Spirit against sin,

17

disease, demons, fear, and every negative force you ever face. He did all this in His physical, visible form, voluntarily accepting all the limitations of the flesh—of being in only one place at a time, being there at one period of time, and of being subject to death. So you see because He voluntarily limited himself, He used only what is available to you and me in our limited human state—and this is FAITH in God and in God's holy Word, which is what I call "Seed-Faith." Jesus said that if you can have faith . . . as a seed, you can say to this mountain, be removed, and it will obey you (Matthew 17:20).

Next, He said that EVERYTHING He did was by the power of the Holy Spirit, saying flatly that He did NOTHING of himself (John 5:19). Likewise, we can do nothing of ourselves; we are totally dependent today on the Spirit . . . HE IS OUR SOURCE.

In order to become man He had to accept human limitations. However, through His faith and His dependence on the Holy Spirit He refused to allow those limitations to defeat Him or to make impossible what He wanted to do. Through the Holy Spirit He moved in both the natural realm AND the supernatural realm. He tried to teach the 3 KEYS to His disciples so they could do it, too.

For 3 years His twelve disciples were by His side—observing, learning, attempting to do as He taught and as He did, and to make the 3 KEYS their way of life. And, amazingly, they learned how, through their faith, they could do MANY of the miracles Jesus did—moving IN and OUT of the miracle realm as easily as He did (Luke 10:17). And when they did, they were unstoppable. They did the IMPOSSIBLE! Yet, when they failed to apply the 3 KEYS they immediately got out of harmony with Jesus. They felt discord between the natural and the supernatural.

What happened? . . .

THEIR EXPECTANCY FOR MIRACLES
WAS OFTEN—AND FINALLY BROKEN

We know of no greater failures in history than these men who were the first to be called Jesus' disciples—men who healed, men who delivered people from demons, men whose words were power, men who knew peace of soul and peace of mind, men who changed others—*these men fell apart like so many of us do today* (John 20:19). AND THEY DID IT WHILE DOING WHAT MOST CHRISTIANS WISH THEY HAD THE PRIVILEGE OF DOING TODAY—WHILE LIVING IN THE PHYSICAL, VISIBLE PRESENCE OF JESUS CHRIST ON EARTH!

You want to see Jesus on earth? . . .   They did.

You want to touch His physical body with your hands? . . .   They did.

You want to be taught by Him physically, face-to-face, actually hearing His words fall upon your ear? . . .   They did.

You wish to live with Him as He was in His human form? . . .   They did.

YET, EVEN THOUGH THEY WERE WITH HIM IN THE FLESH, THEY STILL BECAME MISERABLE FAILURES. HIS PHYSICAL PRESENCE WITH THEM DID NOT SUDDENLY MAKE THEM BECOME SUPERMEN!

At one time they walked out on Him, deserting Him like rats deserting a sinking ship. One even denied he had ever seen, heard, touched, lived with, or known Him . . . after knowing Him as the best friend, in the most personal way possible (Matthew 26:56,70).

Why? . . . Why? . . .

19

Because the physical, visible is never enough . . . NOT THEN . . . NOT NOW . . . NOT EVER! . . .

Next, let's talk about His RETURN TO HEAVEN. Jesus spent 3 years teaching them—OH! How He taught them! When it became obvious that they could not grasp His teachings, THE HOLY SPIRIT HAD TO TAKE THE SECOND STEP (John 16:7; Acts 1:9), which was to *remove Jesus in His physical, visible form from the earth— that form with its voluntary human limitations.* Understanding spiritual truths had to go beyond their physical senses: sight, touch, smell, hearing, feeling, into the dimension of the Holy Spirit himself. The Holy Spirit had been WITH THEM, Jesus told them, but . . . "[He] shall be IN you" (John 14:16,17).

He began to speak of His coming death in terms of being freed from His limited body, and of becoming unlimited in divine power forever through the Resurrection. He said it was better for Him in His physical, visible form to go away, otherwise the Comforter would not come (John 16:7). The Comforter is the Holy Spirit and is translated in the original Greek, PARACLETE. Now don't let that word scare you—it merely means ONE CALLED ALONGSIDE TO HELP. In fact, don't worry about understanding all of this —even Jesus' disciples didn't catch on until *after* Jesus went back to heaven and then sent the Holy Spirit. As you read and reread this, the Holy Spirit will help you to understand Him more clearly (John 14:26).

To prepare them (and us) Jesus said:

"In the last day, that great day of the feast, Jesus stood and cried, saying, If any man thirst, let him come unto me, and drink. He that believeth on me, as the scripture hath said, out of his belly shall flow rivers of living water. (But this spake he of the Spirit, which they that believe on him should receive: for the Holy Ghost was not yet given; because that Jesus was not yet glorified)" (John 7:37-39).

The Holy Spirit could NOT come until the physical, visible Jesus was crucified, risen, and glorified. Jesus said, "I will come to you" (John 14:18). In other words, He is saying, "I, the risen, glorified Christ, no longer limited to a physical, visible body; no longer limited *to* and *by* time and space—and to death—I, the full unlimited Christ, will come back to you. The Holy Spirit—My other self, My personal representative—will bring Me back as the spiritual, invisible Christ; yet having retained all the feelings I experienced as a man and for man (Hebrews 4:15). I will always be in the NOW. I will always be where you are" (Matthew 28:20).

Then He added this astonishing statement: "Greater works than these shall he [you] do, because I go unto my Father" (John 14:12). <u>Remember, the reason He returned to His Father was to send the Holy Spirit</u>, the Paraclete (One called alongside to help). The Holy Spirit would remove the human limitations of our Lord and He would come to us personally, unlimited by time and space, not subject to death, and limitless in His eternal riches, power, and glory.

Before I go further, I want to point out a terrible error many Christians fall into—they think Jesus is poor. And thousands of Christians subconsciously believe it is God's will that they be sick, that they suffer financially and socially. They think of a kind of withdrawal from society. This is why we must be careful not to overemphasize the church building itself. If we are not careful we can, inside those four walls, allow ourselves to be separated and removed from the actual world, its problems, and even our own! Anything physical or visible that we use in our wor-

21

ship of God and discipleship is a means to an end, and not an end in itself.

Jesus says that while you are not to be of the world (John 17:16), you are to be IN it!—IN IT. Involved in it. Taking dominion, subduing the earth, as God told man in the beginning (Genesis 1:28). This, of course, takes you beyond the walls of your own church building.

Where do Christians get this poverty syndrome?—this sickness ethic? Perhaps from statements in the Bible which refer only to Jesus in His physical, visible form where He voluntarily limited himself—to be literal about it, when He took our place—statements such as:

"He made himself of no reputation" (Philippians 2:7).

"Foxes have holes, and the birds of the air have nests; but the Son of man hath not where to lay his head" (Matthew 8:20).

"Though He was rich, yet for your sakes became poor, that ye through his poverty might be rich" (2 Corinthians 8:9).

But listen, in His GLORIFIED form—when He re-entered heaven and sat down at the Father's right hand—there, He was reinvested with His eternal riches, reclothed with all power of heaven and earth, with the keys over death, hell, and the grave, and reendowed with the glory He had before the foundation of the earth.

No longer is our Lord Jesus Christ of no reputation.

No longer is He poor. He did all this for our sakes. Therefore, as the risen Lord, He is qualified to meet our needs while we are still human on this earth. He comes to us IN THE NOW and directly at the point of our need ...

with His original heavenly riches to supply our financial needs ...

22

with His original divine power to heal and strength-
en us in our weaknesses . . .

with His original glory to raise us from obscurity
and nothingness . . .

with His warm loving personal presence for our
loneliness . . .

with His enduement with "power from on high" . . .

with His "now-ness" so that we need never look back
to that physical, visible limited form of 2,000
years ago, but "sit with Him in heavenly places"
. . . in the NOW! . . .

and with His eternal *riches* and *power* and *glory*
available to us every moment.

Since He took on himself our limitations, went to the
cross, rose from the dead, ascended, and poured out the
Holy Spirit, we can have ALL OUR NEEDS MET according to His riches in glory by Christ Jesus (Philippians
4:19). With his eternal resources we can face our limitations with hope and expectation for miracles, many miracles. We know now that we don't have to accept them as
we would have, had Jesus not come in the flesh and taken
our place.

HOW CAN THIS BE?

How can you cross this last frontier of miracles? And
how can YOU know YOU can? The WHO that makes it
possible is the living CHRIST *IN* YOU, through the Holy
Spirit—the glorified, unlimited Lord. He is here. He's here
in the NOW!

Listen, say to yourself over and over, "Christ is in the
NOW!"

Say, "If He is not here in the NOW—He has never
been."

Say, "He is willing to help *me*."

Say, "If He is not willing to help me, He has not been willing to help anybody. But He is ...and He Will!"

This means that God is in your total life—physical, material, spiritual.

YOU HAVE A 7-DAY-A-WEEK LIFE ...

7-day-a-week needs...

You have a 7-day-a-week faith.

YOU HAVE GOD WITH YOU EVERY MOMENT, EVERY DAY, EVERYWHERE, more than those people who saw Him and knew Him in the flesh.

There is another reason WHY GOD IS CLOSER TO YOU NOW ... it is because in this highly mechanized society you need Him to be closer. Life today is more complicated—it's tougher. For example, science has so far outstripped what we have become accustomed to (such as putting men on the moon) that our minds haven't caught up. We feel fear, dread, even shock to our systems. Some call it "future shock." Really, it's PRESENT SHOCK!

But the risen Christ is here in this moment of your existence. His "now-ness" and "near-ness" to you is what makes the difference. Talk about excitment, this is the most exciting of all!

He is not an IT—not a THING—not a particular place.

He is THE MAN HIMSELF ...

Jesus Christ the Person ...

(*Person* in the sense that He is not divided, fragmented, or bruised, as we all are, but a completely whole Person.)

Jesus Christ, your personal Savior ...

Jesus Christ, your Lord ...

24

Jesus Christ, your Source of Total Supply!

So you see how Jesus Christ brings all things together, the spiritual and the material, making you fit in both realms and making both realms fit you. Therefore, during those times your humanness breaks down and you need a miracle, you can have it through Christ WHO is IN you.

THE MOST IMPORTANT THING IN YOUR LIFE IS A MIRACLE . . . ESPECIALLY WHEN YOU NEED ONE

According to Jesus it is the most natural thing in the world for you to move into the miracle realm. God made you this way. Being made in the image of God, and yet man, you have access—direct access—by God's divine laws to take it, to accept it, to move and live in it. Because, as St. Paul says:

"IN HIM WE LIVE, AND MOVE, AND HAVE OUR BEING" (Acts 17:28).

So don't cut God out of your life. If you do, you cut out the divine part of you—the life-giving part of you. Open yourself up to Him as your Lord, both your Savior and your Source of Total Supply for every area of your life, in the here and now—your salvation, your health, your financial supply, your peace of mind, your ability. Let God into your life so it will not erode into nothingness—emptiness—a meaningless vacuum. God wants you to have "things." He's even promised you "all things" for your life on earth (Luke 12:31). But make things instruments rather than your Source—only God can be your Source. Keep a proper balance between things and people, which are instruments only, and God who, alone, is your Source. Speaking personally, I believe this is the best lesson I'm learning as I become a better disciple (follower) of my

25

Lord—of looking on people and things as instruments, BUT UPON GOD AS MY SOURCE.

Often when I feel stress or want and the devil tempts me to look to some person or group or thing for my help, I say, "They're not my Source . . . God is my Source. I must look to Him." Believe me, this really helps to keep my thinking straight and scriptural.

Now I want to tell you about a woman who, by using the 3 KEYS, tapped the miracle realm and got her deepest need met.

HERE IS THE ACTUAL STORY THAT HAPPENED DURING ONE OF OUR TV PROGRAMS AT THE NBC STUDIO— HOW THIS WOMAN LEARNED TO SEED FOR HER MIRACLE IN THE NOW!

Recently, while taping one of our television programs at the NBC Studios in Burbank, California, Wanda, the wife of my producer, brought a woman for prayer who had suffered for years with migraine headaches.

Wanda said, "Oral, people who don't suffer with migraines don't know the hell that those who do, have to endure. This woman is a close friend of mine. She goes to the Presbyterian church, where we go. She's a terrific Christian but she is literally shattered with these headaches. I hope you don't mind our bringing her—we had hoped that perhaps you would have a moment to offer a prayer for her healing."

I said, "Wanda, that's fine. Just have her sit with the audience while Richard and Patti and the World Action Singers sing . . . and then listen to my message on SEED-FAITH. Tell her to really listen . . . and then open her mind to miracles."

After the taping I talked for a few moments with

Only one who has suffered the agony of a migraine can know the torture one goes through ...

Wanda and her friend. As I looked at her I saw the effects of migraine in her face. I felt it in her spirit. I saw what Wanda meant when she said, "She's shattered."

As a man, I've never had many headaches—perhaps a dozen in my entire life. A few were really "splitting headaches." I recalled some of these as I looked at her, remembering the pain that almost split my head open. She talked of the days that a migraine struck and how it stayed with her, virtually paralyzing her personality and being. The medical people were nearly at the end of their rope in treating her. Her children were suffering with her . . . but seemingly nothing lasting could be done.

There are all kinds of ideas about migraines—but so far, people who suffer from them just seem to go on suffering ...

27

Looking at her, I saw in my mind's eye all the people who are ill and who need a miracle. They are being increasingly helped by medical science, but for some unfathomable reason untold thousands still suffer torments that won't leave.

HOW DO YOU EXPLAIN A MIRACLE?

A miracle is not always the same to all people. A miracle to one person might not be a miracle to another. To most of us, a miracle is something happening that we can't explain but that makes a profound change for the better in our lives.

I'm sure that many who hear of a migraine being cured might not call this a miracle—not so with the person who receives the cure. To be free from these excruciating headaches and to be able to live a normal life again is CERTAINLY, IN THEIR MINDS, A MIRACLE. They are not concerned what people think about miracles, they're just glad they have received theirs.

A migraine is like any affliction, or problem, or impossibly tough situation that won't yield to human skill or concern. I say again, the need of a miracle is possibly the most important thing in your life . . . ESPECIALLY WHEN YOU NEED ONE.

MIRACLES ARE THE LAST FRONTIER
YOU MUST CROSS . . . AND YOU CAN.

THE 3 KEYS WERE BEGINNING TO BREAK THROUGH!

As we talked, I saw a gleam of hope in her eyes even through the pain. The 3 KEYS were beginning to break through—especially Key No. 2: Seed for your miracle or, as Jesus said in Luke 6:38, "Give, and it shall be given unto you."

When she came to the taping session, one thought was in her mind: *I've done everything the doctors have told me; if there's something to divine healing I want it.* Back of her mind was the thought: *Oh, if this man of God will only touch me—if God will heal me through his prayers, how grateful I will be!* But now I could tell she was grasping the key of GIVING FIRST, or "seeding for a miracle."

After we had talked for a moment she quickly said, "Mr. Roberts, after hearing your sermon this morning on Philippians 4:15 about giving and receiving, I realized I had the cart before the horse. I thought I had to *receive* before I could *give*. But you are saying, 'God expects me to put a seed in, a seed of faith, that I've got to give God something to work with. I've got to give it to Him first, and it shall be given and multiplied back to me ... '"

I said, "Yes. That's right."

And then she wanted my prayers, which I freely was willing to do. But I surprised her by saying:

"Let's have a two-way prayer, the scriptural way to pray for one another's healing."

She looked at me and I knew she was wondering why. I quoted the Scripture: *Pray one for another that YOU may be healed* (James 5:16). That is, you, the one doing the praying for the other one, are actually praying that you yourself may be healed. Then . . . like a bomb was dropped, she understood! RECEIVING IS THROUGH GIVING! GIVE FIRST. PRAY FOR SOMEONE ELSE FIRST. OPEN UP YOUR INSIDES IN LOVE AND HOPE AND FAITH TO OTHERS FIRST. This was opposite to what she had grown up to believe and accept. (And remember, she was a Christian and hadn't understood the Second Key before.)

Then she said, "This is really new to me, but I can see

29

it's really not new at all. It's in the Bible."

But there was another thing puzzling her and I have to admit the same thing has often perplexed me. It's what Jesus said in Matthew 10:8, "Freely ye have received, freely give."

I said, "What Jesus is saying is that you are to freely give of what He has already given you. What has He given you, or each of us? He said there are only three things that abide in this world: FAITH, HOPE, and LOVE (1 Corinthians 13:13). These are eternal because they are what God is himself, so what God freely gives to you is what He is himself. Therefore, you have FAITH, HOPE, AND LOVE—at least a portion of them in the reservoir of your heart. God has not put them there to stay but to be freely given. *As you give them, they are seed and God multiplies them.*"

As she pondered this, I recalled my own struggle with it.

I said, "As for Jesus telling us to freely give, He is telling you to be Christlike, to be like Him. Being LIKE HIM IS WHERE LIFE IS. And He always gave FIRST."

"God so loved . . . that He gave . . . " (John 3:16).

Giving is love acted out on the human level. It is God happening through us to somebody else. When you convey or transmit love through what you give, you are SEEDING FOR A MIRACLE FOR YOURSELF! And you are doing it on the most practical level. On the earth. Where you hurt the most. Now.

I could understand that she was wondering, with her head splitting with pain right now, how could she give anything. I could tell she was aching inside to change—to start giving . . . AND to be healed in the process by our Lord. I knew too she was on the threshold of crossing the last frontier—the frontier of miracles.

Then we all joined hands for the two-way prayer and

30

she said a little prayer, as I suggested, for me and all the people in the world who are suffering. And pretty soon I could see that she was beginning to feel something. She said, "There's a warmth flooding my whole being—I feel the presence of God. Oh!" she exclaimed, "Mr. Roberts, I'm a different woman. I don't know *how* I'm different, but I *know* I'm a different woman..."

She was back at the studio the next day. And she was, indeed, a different woman. I received a letter from her not long ago and she is still healed and enjoying a new life. Here is a portion of her letter:

Dear Mr. Roberts:

I'm the woman for whom you prayed at the NBC studio several weeks ago. After 20 years of slowly being destroyed by pain and drugs, I've been free of them both since I saw you! I'm raising three children alone...now I can be a real mother to them; so you see, four lives were salvaged, not just one.

I want you to know that Seed-Faith has become a real way of life for me. How can I tell you all that it's done? There's no need too small or large that God hasn't taken care of for us... that's beautiful, but the greatest miracle that's come out of Seed-Faith is the JOY God has added to our lives! The extra dividend of Seed-Faith... the great fringe benefit...is FUN! It's FUN to get up every morning and think, What's the good thing that'll happen today? Maybe that sounds too frivolous, but I'm pretty sure it's the way God wants us to live!

31

*...God really is a happy God, isn't He?
But I never knew before how many wonderful sur-
prises He has for His children...*

*Mr. Roberts, I'm so grateful for the thoughts
you GAVE me and for the teaching to GIVE FIRST,
to seed for my miracles, so that I can receive...
a few minutes' contact with your shining faith
gave me enough to pass on to a great many others...*

Bless you, my dear friend,

Sincerely,

M. H.

M. H. received her miracle in the NOW by learning HOW to seed for a miracle by giving first. And I am telling you, Friend, YOU can do the same thing. HOW? Let me tell you how I learned . . .

AT ONE TIME IN MY LIFE I PERSONALLY COULDN'T BELIEVE JESUS HAD LIVED, much less that He lives in the NOW. I lived as if He didn't exist. I had faith but I didn't put it in Jesus Christ. I put it in myself and in other people. I put it in taking my life into my own hands, of doing things my way. The Bible was like a blurrr to me—its words meaningless as far as I was concerned. I didn't consciously pray. It didn't enter my mind to deliberately turn my life over to God, to have faith in Him as my personal Lord and Savior, or to be filled with the Holy Spirit, or to use my faith as a seed I plant.

As for expecting miracles, I felt I could make my own and I made some, at least they appeared to be. I did a lot of things that excited me. Then one day—

I RAN OUT OF LIFE

I'll never forget, as a young man far from home, when

this happened to me. Like a car out of gas—I couldn't go any further. Life had stalled for me.

With bleeding lungs and hemorrhaging almost daily, I simply RAN OUT OF LIFE. WHERE WAS MY OWN POWER TO MAKE MIRACLES? TO CONTROL MY LIFE? TO REACH THE HEIGHTS? TO DO IT ALL MYSELF?

"No Man Can Ever Make His Own Miracles . . . "

One day I woke up on the *inside*. It dawned on me and I understood it for the first time—*God had permitted me to try to make my own miracle and was showing me that I had failed.* Although I was young, I began to understand NO MAN CAN EVER MAKE HIS OWN MIRACLE. Somewhere—sometime—he *must* come to the end of himself and establish a personal relationship with God, the Source of all miracles. And out of this powerful new understanding, *I repented of my sins* and received Jesus Christ as my personal Savior.

I received the baptism in the Holy Spirit with...
> the new language...
> > of prayer and praise!!!

I learned how to communicate personally with God from my inner self . . . I learned to pray "in the Spirit" and then "with the understanding" (1 Corinthians 14:15).

Later, God revealed to me His promise for the whole of my life:

"You are to take My healing power to YOUR generation . . . "

When I received Christ as my personal Savior and Lord, a transformation began in me. I could feel it. Vibrations of His presence surged through me. I TURNED ON TO MIRACLES. A miracle of healing opened my lungs and loosed my stammering tongue. LIFE flowed up within my inner being. I experienced joy. Enthusiasm for life. Love for people. It never runs dry. It's there all the time. Day and night. Every minute. I wanted to give to others the secret I had learned.

The only failures I've had have come because of my faults, my shortcomings, *or my failure to keep looking to God as the Source of my Total Supply,* or to give first and then to expect miracles. As long as I maintain a commitment of my life to Jesus Christ—

Key No. 1: A commitment to look to Him as MY SOURCE for my Total Supply...

Key No. 2: A commitment that I must SEED for my MIRACLES by giving first . . .

Key No. 3: A commitment to EXPECT MIRACLES from the seeds of faith I put into God's great work...

As long as I follow my Lord in these 3 KEYS OF SEED-FAITH, I have miracle after miracle. Sometimes I get so elated I find myself looking around the corner to see what miracle God is going to give me next!

A TWO-PART PATTERN

Over the years a two-part pattern has formed in which I have seen God work miracles. The first part of the pattern is that weeks or months after I've prayed and seeded for a miracle (and continued to look to my Source for it to happen) then there is my miracle right before my eyes.

The second part of the pattern is that sometimes miracles happen very quickly. It almost stuns me, it's so quick. But to be perfectly frank, most of my miracles do not happen quickly. I'm even tempted to look to an <u>instrument</u> rather than to God my <u>SOURCE</u>. Sometimes I'm tempted to actually believe God has forgotten me, or doesn't care. Sometimes I find myself saying:

"God, WHY? WHY is this happening to me? What have I done to deserve it?"

Then I try to remember that questions like these are the signs of a loser. A winner doesn't dwell on, "Why has this happened to me? What have I done to deserve this?" A winner starts with a different kind of question:

"Am I failing to do what God says in the Bible for me to do to come out of this?"

"Who am I making my Source of Total Supply—man or God?"

"Have I been seeding for a miracle, as God says, 'cheerfully'"?

"Am I demanding that God send my miracle in my own *WAY* and *TIME,* OR AM I TRUSTING HIM AS MY SOURCE TO SEND IT IN *HIS* OWN *TIME* AND *WAY?*"

As I remember the difference between a loser and a winner, then I can try to do something about my situation. It helps me take action in a positive direction—God's. I try not to sit (or lie) there asking negative question after negative question, eating my heart out, increasing my misery. Taking action like this has been a great help to me. It has helped me receive many miracles that people had told me were impossible. I'm learning a fierce, tenacious expectation for my miracle to happen . . . and at the same time, to really trust God my Source to make my miracle happen in His own WAY and TIME. It's not always easy to do this—I have to consciously and prayerfully work at it.

Friend, you can't change God but you can let HIM change YOU. I know of no better way to begin than by starting to faithfully use the 3 KEYS for your miracles.

I have a feeling you need one, A BIG ONE, right now.

NOTES

3

HOW TO MAKE GOD THE SOURCE OF YOUR TOTAL SUPPLY

A BIG BRAWNY HULK OF A GUY sat across from me. A look of anguish was on his face. Physically, he appeared to be a tower of strength and health. Yet I could see that look of despair in his eyes—that he wanted to open his heart and tell me something. His problem was physical and financial, and I sensed right away that beneath there was a deeper problem; and, like all problems, it was spiritually based. I knew it, but he didn't.

"My insides are hurting," he blurted.

"Who is your Source?" I asked.

"I go to church," he said.

"Who do you trust?" I asked.

"Well, I guess I don't know what you mean," he answered in puzzlement.

"WHO IS YOUR SOURCE?" I asked the third time. "Everybody trusts someone or something—but not always GOD."

"Oh, I trust in God, Mr. Roberts."

"Then how can you be hurting inside?" I smiled. "Don't be surprised at my questions. They're the ones I ask myself. I, too, hurt inside sometimes."

"You do?"

"Oh, yes. Then I have to start where you are today, asking myself, 'Who do I trust?'"

"Well, Oral Roberts, who do you trust?"

"Well," I said, "I've trusted in people and many have helped me, but when I have a real need and I call on people, usually—nine times out of ten—they let me down."

"Me, too," he said.

"I've trusted in things and often found them helpful, but at the point where I have a real problem I see just how limited things are to help me. THE GREAT MOMENT IN MY LIFE IS WHEN I BEGIN TO AWAKEN TO WHO THE SOURCE OF MY TOTAL SUPPLY REALLY IS— ONE WHOM I CAN TRUST ALL THE WAY—ONE WHO CAN BRING THE MIRACLE I NEED INTO MY LIFE— GOD."

He looked at me and began nodding his head. I said, "Yes, I believe in people. Also, I appreciate and use things, but what I really try to do is trust completely in God. God is the only One who has never let me down.

I've found God is . . .

    too wise to make a mistake . . .

      too good to do wrong . . .

        too strong to fail."

He thought a moment and said, "You're trying to say something to me, aren't you?"

"Yes. I feel your spirit. Your spirit is the real you."

"What do you feel in me? Go ahead, tell me. I want to know."

"I'm glad you're opening up," I said. "For unless you want to know the truth of God about yourself, you'll never know who you trust and you'll never stop this awful hurting inside."

Looking at him, I said, "I sense that you are listening with your fears and reacting with your doubts."

"Well, I know I have some fears and doubts. Doesn't everybody?"

"Yes, more or less, but Jesus taught us to doubt our doubts, to reject our fears, and to believe our faith. For example, Jesus said:

'If thou canst believe, all things are possible to him that believeth' (Mark 9:23).

'Fear not: believe only' (Luke 8:50).

As thou hast believed, so be it done unto thee' (Matthew 8:13).

And Hebrews 11:6 tells us:

'He that cometh to God must believe that he is, and that he is a rewarder of them that diligently seek him.'

Now all these things the Bible says to show us whom we can trust, who our Source is, and how we can turn all our faith toward Him—rather than trusting only in people and things. Then we can find abundant life."

"You talk a lot about Jesus bringing abundant life, don't you?" he said.

"Yes, I do. Jesus said, 'I am come that they might have life, and that they might have it more abundantly' (John 10:10). Remember, when Jesus spoke those words, the world was filled with impossibilities. In fact, things were not much different than they are today. All around Him,

Jesus saw people hemmed in by circumstances, disease, discrimination, poverty, fear, and failure. And He knew that in heaven there are resources for man's needs—

> water for his thirst,
> food for his hunger,
> strength for his weakness,
> riches for his poverty,
> a kiss for his sorrow,
> gladness for his misery, and
> love for his loneliness.

So Jesus reached up and took heaven and kissed the earth with it, and opened it and gave to the children of men. He came with outstretched hands filled with God's blessing, with an open heaven behind Him. He came into people's lives at the point of their need, performing miracles and setting them free. *Jesus Christ the same yesterday, and to day, and for ever* (Hebrews 13:8).

What He was then, He is NOW.

He opened heaven then, He is opening heaven NOW.

He's opening it for you.

"THIS ABUNDANT LIFE THAT JESUS GIVES IS A LIFE-FORCE THAT MAKES AN INDIVIDUAL FEEL ALIVE AND GIVES HIM A RHYTHM OF FAITH AND SUCCESS. IT DOES SOMETHING TO THE INSIDES OF HIS BEING. It's like a river flooding up from the inner man. And Jesus alone brings this abundant life. He is the Source of your Total Supply. He is the One we are to trust."

My friend thought this over a moment. Then he said, "Mr. Roberts, you say it does something to the inside of a man. Well, I'm hurting in my insides. I want what you're talking about."

"You *really* want it?" I asked.

"Yes, I want it with all my heart. What I've been through shows me that I'm not sure who I trust, as you put it. For the first time, I'm beginning to realize that I've not been looking to God as my Source. I guess I've looked to people and things. And I suppose I have tried to be sort of a source to myself, perhaps even trying to make my own miracles."

"My brother," I said, "now you're getting onto the right track. God says the day that you seek Him with all your heart, that's the day you will find Him" (Deuteronomy 4:29).

"Well, that's what I want to do—to find God. Then I know I'll be a new man."

"When you came in here you were pretty sure you had all the faith you needed. Then you responded to the question, 'Who do you trust?' Now you see just how far you are from trusting in God, how vague He is to you as your Source. That's good—real good. Now you can start where you are—right where you are hurting—and Jesus will meet you there."

The Holy Spirit was really dealing with him. He asked, "But how? How?"

I said, "I think you should go back to the Bible. Start with what God says. When you read and study the Bible, try to realize that the Bible is God talking directly to you. It will help if you'll stop every now and then and write your name so you'll feel that God is talking to you. WHEN I HOLD THE BIBLE IN MY HANDS AND READ, I FEEL IN THE DEEPEST PART OF MY BEING THAT GOD IS TALKING TO ME—*ORAL ROBERTS*. HE IS DEALING WITH ME AS A PERSON. So when I find myself hurting inside (as you say you are) I go back to my guidebook, the Bible, and back to my SOURCE, GOD. I start there."

He had listened intently. Now he said, "Seeing you on television and reading your books and magazines, I see that you have organized your thinking and your life along a definite pattern. I often hear you talking about *the 3 KEYS of Seed-Faith* that you live by. You make it sound simple, but is it really simple?"

"All great truths are simple, if we only knew it. Concerning the 3 KEYS of Seed-Faith, I've already referred to the first key in asking you, WHO DO YOU TRUST or WHO IS THE SOURCE OF YOUR TOTAL SUPPLY? The Bible says, *My God shall supply all your need according to his riches in glory by Christ Jesus* (Philippians 4:19). (This is Key No. 1—start now—memorize it. Make it a part of your being.) You've got to have a Source for your life—God. The Bible also says:

'Thou shalt have no other gods before me' (Exodus 20:2).

'Bless the Lord, O my soul, and forget not all his benefits: Who forgiveth all thine iniquities; who healeth all thy diseases . . . who crowneth thee with lovingkindness and tender mercies; Who satisfieth thy mouth with good things' (Psalm 103:2-5).

"Also Jesus said, '*I am the way,* the truth and the life.'

"So you see, everything begins with God; He is your Source, all others are instruments only."

Then I said, "I am continually asked, 'Oral Roberts, how do you support such a tremendous operation as ORU and national weekly and quarterly telecasts—the tremendous expenses?' I frankly admit there are times when my back is to the wall because of a financial need. When this happens I am tempted sometimes to run to people—to friends who might help us. But then God calms me down and I am reminded that He alone is my Source. God uses people, but they are instruments only. GOD IS MY SOURCE. When I look to Him for my supply, the miracle happens and our needs are met. God sees to that!"

As we were talking I sensed a change taking place in my friend. Suddenly he said, "You know, my insides are not hurting anymore. I feel good."

I said, "You feel like you can go with God and get your needs met, don't you?"

He said, "I sure do."

Friend, let me ask you, just as I asked this man, WHO DO YOU TRUST? WHO IS THE SOURCE OF YOUR TOTAL SUPPLY?

Remember: When you trust without question, that is real trust. So you must start with Key No. 1 of Seed-Faith, "Who do I trust? Who is my Source?"

> You can start where you are now—
> right where you are hurting—
> and THE MAN JESUS CHRIST YOUR LORD
> will meet you there.
> Everything begins with Him. He is your
> Source.for the miracle you need; all
> others are instruments only
> (Philippians 4:19). (Key No. 1.)

Open your mind . . . start trying to get your thoughts on God—of looking to Him as the Source of your Total Supply and of making Seed-Faith living your way of life. Try. Try. Try. I promise you God is going to bless you as you've never known before.

NEVER DOUBT THE POWER OF YOUR OWN FAITH, NEVER, NEVER, NEVER!

NOTES

Often Evelyn and I start the morning by reading your letters at the breakfast table and praying for God to meet all your needs.

4 HOW TO SEED FOR YOUR MIRACLE

ONE MORNING MY WIFE EVELYN and I were sitting at breakfast, going through our mail, when she picked up a letter and said:

"Oral, you've got to listen to this . . ." and she read:

Dear Brother Roberts:

By the time this letter reaches you I WILL HAVE TRIED TO COMMIT SUICIDE UNLESS A MIRACLE HAPPENS IN THE MEANTIME. I know that God does not give us a cross too heavy to carry, but even Jesus fell three times on the way to Calvary. Each time, He managed to get up until the end. I, too, have

45

reached the end. My husband left me with five
small children and no support. Now within a period
of a month we have had measles, scarlet fever,
pneumonia, and one child has had surgery.

The woman my husband lives with has children
but they are all well and happy. Why does God let
them be happy? Why does it have to be my children
who suffer? We are on welfare and there is never
enough to eat. How do you think I feel when my
children ask for a bowl of cereal and I have to
say, "We don't have any." They want a glass of
milk and I have to say, "You will have to drink
water. We don't have any milk." This hurts me so
bad. What do I do, Brother Roberts?

Now, don't write me a letter with God's direct
Word from the Bible. Just answer in plain everyday
words like the world we live in, so I can understand.
I wrote this letter to you just as I would talk to
you if I were with you face-to-face. And that's
the kind of answer I want back from you...

Evelyn was deeply disturbed about this woman's problems and she said, "Oral, what will you say to her? How
can you answer this?"

And I said, "Honey, I'll have to speak to her from the
Bible, from what Jesus says. I really cannot speak for myself . . . I will first give her the words of Jesus in Mark
12:41-44. *And Jesus sat over against the treasury [of the
temple], and beheld how the people cast money into the
treasury: and many that were rich cast in much. And there
came a certain poor widow, and she threw in two mites [or
pennies] . . . And he called unto him his disciples, and saith
unto them, Verily I say unto you, That this poor widow hath*

46

cast more in, than all they which have cast into the treasury:
For all they did cast in of their abundance; but she of her
want did cast in all that she had, even all her living.

Evelyn said, "Well, what is there in that Scripture that speaks to this woman?"

I said, "Look, this woman who wrote us is at the end of her rope. Everything has gone wrong. She doesn't have anything left. What can she do? She now has no husband. What can I say to her? Absolutely nothing. But our Jesus, our Lord and Source, can say something to her.

"The Bible says that one day He was sitting in the temple watching the people give. He saw the people come up who had a lot and He seemed to appreciate that they would give from their abundance. But when the little widow came, Jesus turned to His disciples and said, 'She has given the most!'

SHE CAST IN OF HER WANT

"When the disciples wanted to know why, Jesus explained, 'Because they cast in of their abundance . . . of their surplus. They won't really miss what they have given. It was something that wasn't costing them anything, but this widow CAST IN OF HER WANT.' "

Evelyn said, "Say that again."

"She cast in of her WANT . . . of her need. Of what she was desperately fighting for. She cast in of her want and Jesus said, 'She cast in the most.' "

And these are the thoughts I shared with this woman in my letter to her: God appreciates all our gifts, but

real Bible giving has to come
from the core of your being.

It has to speak of yourself—your time, your talent, your love, your earnings, your whole personality, your very soul.

47

When this little widow woman gave her two mites—all that she had—they were by-products of her heart which is the reservoir into which God puts all He gives to us. Jesus saw this when her hands put in the two mites. She needed many mites (money). From this need, her *heart* was giving.

SEEDING FOR A MIRACLE (This is Key No. 2.)

She was putting in seed, something that desperately cost—something of herself. And Jesus saw it and was *excited* about the widow's gift.

Today people would say, "That's terrible that Jesus would accept her gift, a gift that was all she had." But He accepted it as seed that she planted that He might multiply it back to meet all her needs. He was doing her a favor when He accepted her *little* so He could give to her of His *much*.

You see, Jesus said, "It is more blessed [or *productive*] to give than to receive."

WHY?

Because it is in giving that you can receive back.

WHY?

Because what you give is the seed you put in; the seed is the only thing God can multiply back. In other words, only seed sown can result in a harvest. While the widow held the two mites—they were just that, two mites—only when she gave them to Jesus could they be multiplied.

WHY is giving a source of continual increase in your goods, your time, your talent, your health, your spiritual growth?

Because God put RECEIVING in giving. It is like the yeast in bread. The dough is not multiplied until the yeast in it becomes the multiplying agent. He made giving the multiplying agent of that which you give. Your giving ties you to God. It links you to the inexhaustible Source of life itself, ABUNDANT LIFE. This is God's world and you are your Father's child. He loves you. He gave His only Son to die in your place. In your giving back to Him . . .

You are touching God at His very heart.

You are opening the floodgates of His supply for all your needs.

You are opening the door to His own riches.

"But my God shall supply all your need according to His riches in glory" (Philippians 4:19).

The Bible says, "He became poor for our sake that we might become rich," or as *The Living Bible* puts it, "Though he was so very rich, yet to help you he became so very poor, so that by being poor he might make you rich" (2 Corinthians 8:9).

In other words, He divested himself, or laid aside His riches in heaven, for our sake—to help us. Why? First, to identify with us in every area of our human need, such as the physical, spiritual, financial, and material. He did it to help us. It was part of what He suffered for us as He voluntarily limited himself to live in a physical, visible form. But through His death on the cross and His Resurrection He returned to His Father, to sit on His right hand where the Father reinvested Him with His eternal power, reclothed Him with His eternal glory, and reendowed Him with His eternal riches. He picked up again what He had laid aside—His riches, power and glory. So that now, as the Source of our Total Supply, He has promised to supply all your need according to His riches IN GLORY BY CHRIST JESUS (Philippians 4:19).

So you see, it's wrong to "glory" in poverty or to link poverty with our Lord in His present unlimited form—

poverty in any form that would limit us in having our needs met. The Scriptures speak of Jesus' present glorified position in heaven, saying that we have all sufficiency in Him (2 Corinthians 9:8).

It was a good day in my life when the Holy Spirit began to open this eternal truth up to me about my Lord. I want you to read the preceding paragraphs again and again— until the Spirit illumines your mind with it. Then it will be a great day in your life, too.

Because our Lord Jesus Christ IS in His glory with all the everlasting riches and power and glory fully restored to Him through His Resurrection and glorification, and because through the Holy Spirit He is with us in the NOW, He is not limited to time or space or lack of any kind. He is where you are—wherever you are—and there to help you in ways even above what you can ask or think (Ephesians 3:20).

Again I say THE SECRET OF LIFE is in expecting miracles from our risen Lord. Show me a person who does not expect miracles from God and there's no way he can have the zing of life, or the fullness of life, or get his real needs met.

THE PRESUMPTUOUSNESS OF LIFE is in expecting a miracle when there's no possible way to get one, because if we do not put the seed in, we do not give God anything to work with.

The Bible way to receive a miracle is to first start giving God something to work with. To give as Jesus gave—something that costs, something that touches you at the core of your being. Giving out of your WANT, as the poor widow gave (Mark 12:41-44).

If you are out of time, you give some of it.

If you want friendship desperately, that's what you give.

If you need money to pay your bills, take some of what you have and give it to our Lord and His work.

This is what excites Jesus for you are giving of your *want*.

YOU ARE SEEDING FOR A MIRACLE

This is one of the major differences between Old Testament and New Testament giving. In the Old Testament you gave *after* you received—you paid tithe—you gave the tenth to God. But in the New Testament, you seed for your miracle by giving FIRST. Let me explain:

In the Old Testament, God spoke to a group of people and led them into the land of promise and He gave them certain laws and regulations. In order to separate them from the nations of the world and dedicate them to himself, He tried to teach them His ownership. Therefore, He said, *Bring all the tithe into the storehouse.*

The tenth dollar is God's . . .

The seventh day is God's . . .

The firstborn son is God's.

They received first and then they gave the tenth, the seventh day, the firstborn son—they gave all these back to God. They gave it because it was a debt they owed.

Eventually the debt of what we owed to God was too big for any man to pay, so God gave His Son Jesus Christ as the seed of David. He gave Him to go to the cross to be the divine seed sown. He gave Him to pay the price—to pay the unpayable debt.

CAN WE UNDERSTAND THAT JESUS, THE MAN, had to learn to give to God exactly like you and I do? The writer of Hebrews spoke of His learning obedience, I mean

51

having to <u>learn</u> it like I have to learn it—like you have to learn it. The Bible says, *Though he [Jesus] were a Son, yet LEARNED he obedience by the things which he suf-fered* (Hebrews 5:8).

Eventually Jesus had to face the thing that God wanted Him to do. For "he [Jesus] had offered up prayers and supplications with strong crying and tears unto him that was able to save him from death" (Hebrews 5:7). Jesus, as a man, didn't <u>want</u> to go to the cross. He didn't <u>want</u> nails driven into His hands.

Can you imagine how much that would hurt? You have a pin to prick you or something to stick you and how you jerk . . . how you hurt. Imagine having the flesh and bones of your hands crunched by a nail being driven through them and nails driven through your feet.

Imagine being stripped and hung there before the crowd, derided and cast out. Jesus didn't look forward to that. He wanted men to understand that He came to the world to save them, but they did not. And He cried for God to grant Him some other way, but there was no other way to be granted, because:

> You must start putting in a seed if you want
> it to be multiplied . . .
> You must start giving in order to receive . . .

That's the eternal law of God. That's the God-given law of nature—and so Jesus had to give. His humanness didn't want to give any more than yours and mine want to give.

I don't think anybody really wants to give unless the gift of God's love is flowing in his life. I think he thinks only of RECEIVING. I think he wants to see how much he can GET . . . then maybe he'll think about giving some of it.

I think we face that problem every day. We want people

to give to us. We don't want to get up and help somebody else. We don't want to smile first. We don't want to pat anybody on the back. We don't want to love. We don't want to pray for others. That's our human nature. In salvation, Jesus gives us a NEW nature (2 Corinthians 5:17). Then He shows us how to follow His example in giving up our own way and taking God's (Luke 9:23). Right there in that terrible experience in Gethsemane, He looked to His Father, the Source of all His life. He saw He could win only by giving himself. Only by giving up His own will or desire to God's higher will, could He bring forth the thing He wanted most: His own life raised from the dead that all others might have hope of salvation and a new life. So Jesus gave of His want, of His need—just as the widow did (the one He said gave the most). For like the widow's mite, His life He gave was all He had. When He finally said, "Not my will, but thine be done," He came into the real spirit of

SEEDING FOR A NEW LIFE

He did this by faith. This is why I keep saying, "Never doubt the power of your own faith." Never. Never.

What followed the cross, the giving of Christ's life? It was the Resurrection! For we could have no resurrection unless Christ had first given His life. And, likewise,

you can have no miracle . . .

no harvest for the meeting of your needs . . .

unless you are willing to plant some seed.

In the New Covenant (or Testament) of our Lord, giving is an opportunity because in the act of giving you are actually sowing a seed—or seeding for your miracle. Giving is the expression of your love—love in action— moving out of self into the way of God, into Seed-Faith giving and receiving, into sowing and reaping.

53

Whatever you give—no matter what form it takes—is a seed you put into Christ's great work of saving mankind. It is a seed for God to use . . .

AND IT IS ALWAYS A SEED FOR GOD TO
MULTIPLY BACK TO YOU!

You—*YOU* put the seed in. YOU initiate the action. The action is God's eternal law of sowing and reaping working in your behalf. The eternal law goes all the way back to Genesis 8:22.

IT HAS NEVER BEEN REPEALED . . .
IT IS AN EVERLASTING COVENANT GOD
MAKES WITH ANY MAN WHO WILL
FOLLOW HIM.

As a disciple of Christ today—in the NOW of your needs and problems—you FOLLOW Jesus—you do what He did. This means YOU love FIRST . . .

You give FIRST . . .
You forgive FIRST . . .
You apologize FIRST . . .
You pray for others FIRST . . .
You smile FIRST . . .
You go the second mile FIRST.

Otis Winters

By doing so you initiate a new action in your situation— YOU "SEED FOR YOUR MIRACLE!"

Otis Winters, a young businessman friend of mine, received a great miracle in his business when he learned this secret. In 1969, I had given him a typed copy of the manuscript of MIRACLE OF SEED-FAITH while it was still being printed. He got real excited about it and later wrote me the following letter:

> Dear Oral:
>
> I just finished your new book's manuscript, Miracle of Seed-Faith, and it has meant a great deal to me. It made me examine my own religious growth, and I believe I am entering a FOURTH STAGE that will be most exciting and rewarding. The three previous (but still learning) stages were:
>
> 1. Accepting Christ as my personal Savior.
>
> 2. Understanding the devil and his program of inflicting doubt, temptation, and aggression; and God's forgiveness again by confessing my sins again. I became active in the church and learned more about the Lord.
>
> 3. Accepting the Holy Spirit as God with us today, empowering me to witness for Jesus.
>
> 4. THE NEW STAGE IS TO UNDERSTAND AND USE THE MIRACLE OF SEED-FAITH...
>
> --Otis Winters

Otis and his wife Ann came to a seminar at Oral Roberts University and heard me speak about the 3 KEYS of Seed-Faith but, in his own words, they "missed the point completely." They made a Seed-Faith pledge that day and went away feeling that they were expecting a miracle.

Later Otis said, "We missed the idea of planting a seed first so God would have something to work with, something to multiply back to us. We were like the city farmers who expected a bountiful harvest from a field that had no seed planted in it, or the soil tilled. We were waiting for a miracle of money and <u>then we would pay our pledge.</u> This should come under the heading of 'tithing' and we <u>owe</u> that to the Lord anyway."

Later I talked with Otis and I sensed that day that he had a great need in his business.

I said, *"Otis, no man will fully follow Jesus Christ successfully until he settles the issue concerning Jesus' relationship with his needs AND WITH HIS GIVING."*

He caught the <u>second key</u>—"Seed for your miracle by giving first." A few days later he wrote a check for God that was truly Seed-Faith giving which started his business on an incredible financial harvest, and more importantly, on a harvest of spiritual change for his soul and the souls of his family.

Otis was in the process of enlarging his business. (His is the business of manufacturing educational teaching tapes.) Money was tight but he felt this was God's direction. He went ahead with expansion plans because he felt he had the financing worked out. Among other things, they had been trying to sell their home.

Within 5 days after planting his Seed-Faith check, he sold his house which had been on the market for 8 months. Then he said, "Two days after we sold our house I learned that my number one prospect had just decided not to invest in our company. This shattered me until I remembered what you said:

'GOD AS OUR SOURCE CONTROLS THE UNEXPECTED SUPPLY AS WELL AS THE EXPECTED.'

"We were fast approaching a deadline when I had to come up with the investors 'or else.' I had 3 weeks left. Five days and a lot of work and prayer later, two new investors were located! (Unexpected? To me, yes, but not to God.) I now had the job of getting three investment companies to agree and sign a contract, as well as release the money, with an *impossible* deadline. With the Lord's help, I managed (even with close friends telling me repeatedly, 'It can't be done!!!') to have the contract signed, WITH 2 MINUTES to spare, so that the money was released in time to save our business.

"They said it couldn't be done but I knew the Lord wanted it done. We sold 32% of the stock in our company for four times the actual book value of our business at that time. This happened in the worst financial market in 40 years. Many persons have expressed amazement but I know it is a miracle of Seed-Faith giving."

So many people hear us talk about GIVING and they immediately send up a red flag! They think money!! Of course, your money represents you. You can't separate your money from you because your money is what you earn by your time and your sweat and your toil. Your money is you but your time is you, too. And your talent is you. And your concern is you.

SEED-FAITH LIVING MEANS YOU GIVE YOURSELF

I think the most difficult thing people have to face in Seed-Faith is when they think it's only a gimmick. For example, they say:

"I'll give a certain amount of money and suddenly everything will be changed." And it doesn't happen—not if it's only used as a gimmick. Seed-Faith must become a way of life. It must bring you to the living Christ so that you turn your life over to Him, trusting Him as the Source of your Total Supply. Then it will really join you WITH

57

the Person, WITH the Man Jesus Christ himself, to follow and be like Him as His disciple every day.

Jesus said, *If any man will come after me, let him deny himself, and take up his cross daily, and follow me* (Luke 9:23). Jesus says this is a "daily" way of life.

Denying yourself and taking up your cross is the giving of yourself. Giving is a sacrifice. Sometimes our giving hurts . . . because we all want to receive first, not give first. This is what Jesus wants to change in us—from wanting to receive first to giving first, as He did. EVERY TIME YOU GIVE, A LITTLE BIT OF YOU DIES. You die to self. A little bit of that part of you that wants to run your life . . . that wants to leave God out and not include others . . . dies. ON THE OTHER HAND, EVERY TIME YOU GIVE OF YOURSELF A LITTLE BIT OF YOU COMES ALIVE, AND YOU SHARE IN THE NOW OF THE RESURRECTION (THE HARVEST) THAT FOLLOWS ON THE HEELS OF THE CROSS. IT'S GOD'S DIVINE LAW OF RETURN.

Remember, *you become a Christian the moment you believe upon Jesus Christ as your Savior. But it takes a lifetime to become a disciple of Jesus . . . a follower and learner of Christ . . . in other words, a Seed-Faith Christian.*

Once you get this straight in your mind, then you can move on into a direction of daily Seed-Faith living. It becomes a joy to give because you know you are seeding for a miracle. You keep giving day by day until giving becomes a part of you . . . giving without grudging . . . giving in joy . . . "for God loveth a cheerful giver" (2 Corinthians 9:7). You give in joy because you are helping others, and because of the harvest you KNOW you will receive. The Bible says, *For the joy that was set before him, [Jesus]*

endured the cross, despising the shame (Hebrews 12:2).
Jesus endured the cross because He saw the Resurrection—
the harvest. He saw His seed-giving multiplied millions
of times in the lives of believers all over the world. If you
are a Christian, you are part of the harvest of the seed
Jesus planted on the cross.

How can you give joyfully?? Hilariously??? Only one
way—because of the living Christ indwelling you and because of the *knowledge* of the harvest! When you give,
God's divine law of return goes into effect and multiplies
the seed sown—the gift given. And it is multiplied back
every time in the form of your hopes and dreams and personal needs.

Listen, Friend, God is not poor; God is not sick. God
is not removed from us. He is LIFE. As a partner with
Him, there is no shortage of any good thing for your life.

Dr. Leney and I at a seminar at ORU

One of my friends
and partners, Dr. Fannie
Lou Leney, is a medical
doctor. She is a special-
ist in treating allergies.
One of the reasons for
her success is that she
quietly prays as she
treats her patients even
though the patient
doesn't know she's pray-
ing. Not long ago she
was up in Kansas visit-
ing some friends, and
while out on the high-
way she ran out of gas.
Pretty soon a great big

gas truck came up and stopped, and the driver said, "Lady, can I help you?"

"Well," she said, "I just would like for you to stop at the next station and tell them to bring me some gas."

"Well," he said, "Woman, I've got 2,000 gallons in my truck right now."

"I understand," she said, "but would you tell someone up there to bring me out three or four gallons."

"Lady, I've got 2,000 gallons right here!"

"You mean you can—"

"Yes, I have a little hose over here. I'll just put it up against this big tank and put it in your little tank and, Lady, I can solve your problem."

"Please do," she said.

And when he had filled up her tank, he smiled and said, "You see, I really won't miss these few little gallons out of this big tank."

Later, when Dr. Leney told me about this, she was elated. She said, "Now I know what you mean.

GOD IS MY SOURCE!

GOD IS MY SOURCE!

"It's not going to diminish God to take something of what He has and put it in my little life."

I said, "Dr. Leney, that's beautiful and it really works."

―――――

I tell you, Friends, God's riches are laid end-to-end across heaven waiting to be given to you. And God is not limited by your circumstances!!!

The BIG question is,
ARE YOU SEEDING FOR A MIRACLE???

Or, are you living a presumptuous life? Are you presuming that God is going to do something in your life when you are not cooperating with Him, when you are not opening up your heart and giving—and giving first?

Think now of your need but don't get problem-centered. That is to say, don't think only of your need and problem. In your mind, transfer from that problem, that need, to the God of eternity and of the NOW. Use the 3 KEYS.

Key No. 1: Open your heart . . . put God first in your life . . . <u>trusting</u> in Him as the Source of your Total Supply.

Key No. 2: Open your mind to a new concept of <u>giving</u>— seeding for your miracle.

Key No. 3: Open your mind to a new concept of <u>receiving</u>—Expect a miracle!

This is the guts, the heart, the soul of Seed-Faith living. This is the message of the gospel. It is the Good News. You put yourself in as seed—no matter how small you feel, or how big your need is, or how difficult your problem, or severe the shortages are in your home. You give of your total self. Then <u>God's divine law of return</u> does the rest. It reproduces a miraculous harvest to meet the needs in your life. It never fails!

Learn the 3 KEYS. Start practicing them today! Just one word characterizes each one.

TRUSTING

SEEDING

EXPECTING

□ □

NOTES

5 HOW TO MAKE YOUR MIRACLE START HAPPENING IN THE NOW

RECENTLY ONE OF OUR ORU BASKETBALL COACHES was up North recruiting, and a coach from a very large high school asked, "Why are you here?"

He replied that he wanted a certain player to visit the ORU campus, and this coach said, "Well, you don't have a prayer."

"Why not?" the ORU coach asked.

He said, "If you could get this outstanding player to visit your little school, it would be a miracle."

And our coach smiled and said:

"THAT JUST HAPPENS TO BE THE AREA
THAT WE WORK IN—MIRACLES."

(You guessed it, the young athlete agreed to come.)

Across the Oral Roberts University are signs which read, "Expect a miracle!" (This is Key No. 3—begin saturating your thinking with these 3 KEYS and put them to work for you.) Miracles are not academic at ORU, they are a reality . . . they are a NECESSITY. The very campus is built upon Seed-Faith and miracles.

In 1962, there were only three small buildings under construction at ORU. When we announced that we planned to build a fully accredited liberal arts university, the skeptics had a heyday. And when we broke ground for the

Learning Resources Center—a $6-million* building—even our friends became fearful. I remember a warm friend said to me, "Oral, you can't do it." And that was all I heard. I heard this from everybody. And from the human standpoint, it couldn't be done. I knew *I* couldn't do it but I knew faith in God, the Source of my Total Supply, could! Pretty soon —

I DIDN'T KNOW IT COULDN'T BE DONE!!!

I'm reminded of the story about the little bumblebee. It is said to be a scientific impossibility for him to fly. His body is too heavy; his wings are too small. But he doesn't know this so he just flies anyway—and makes a little honey as he goes along.

ALL THE SUCCESS OF ANYTHING UNDERTAKEN IN THE NAME OF GOD BEGINS IN THE RECOGNITION OF THE AUTHORITY OF GOD. God is Creator and Lord. God is the Author and Finisher of our faith. He is the Alpha and Omega, the Beginning and End of our existence. He is above all earthly power, all human wisdom. He stands at the edge of the universe, and the center of the earth. He fills this universe with himself and His own divine presence.

I have had to learn personally to come under the authority of God. When I was 17 I accepted Christ as my personal Savior. I should have done it much earlier but I'm sorry to say that I ran away from God, even turning away from my dear godly parents. I became ill with tuberculosis and was brought home to die.

But when I learned that God was concerned about me— Oral Roberts—as a human being, as a young man bleeding

*The Learning Resources Center later grew to a $10-million project, including furnishings.

and hemorrhaging to death from his lungs, that's when I wanted Christ as my Lord. I was converted, born again by the Spirit of God, and received the call to preach the gospel. God said:

"YOU ARE TO TAKE MY HEALING POWER TO YOUR GENERATION"

Some time later God spoke to my heart again and said:

"BUILD ME A UNIVERSITY . . . BUILD IT UNDER MY AUTHORITY AND . . . ON THE HOLY SPIRIT." Now can you imagine a 17-year-old boy being told that? How difficult it was to understand.

I began, not knowing how or where to go, but I began with the love of God in my heart and a concern and compassion for human beings.

I went out to touch people's

This is me shortly after I was healed of tuberculosis . . . lives in the healing name of Jesus Christ. I felt His compassion flowing through me. I prayed for thousands. Sometimes I failed. I made mistakes. But people accepted me because they felt God's love was in my heart and I loved them. That same love flows through me today.

I feel it.

It moves me.

It thrills me.

Through the years as I traveled in five continents ministering to large crowds, I carried the dream that someday in God's own time I would obey His words to build Him a university—not because I thought I knew <u>how</u>. I was prob-

65

ably one of the lesser qualified ones in knowing how to build an academic university—but because He had <u>said</u> to do it, I knew I had to do it to fulfill His larger purpose for my calling to the ministry of healing.

I knew too that the Source of my Total Supply had to be God. I had no other source on this earth.

I knew I had to give of myself, and keep on giving when it all looked so foolish. Only as I continued to put seed in would God multiply it.

And I knew above everything else I had to EXPECT A MIRACLE. Humanly speaking, nothing less than a miracle from God could get the job done.

My constant problem was not to start too quickly, but to be patient and to wait on God's time. All through the '50s I wondered if it was God's time. I even parked my car in front of the pasture where ORU now stands, and with my children I prayed for God to hold that piece of property for us. In the early '60s God spoke to my heart impressing me with:

"NOW'S THE TIME"

As we sought ways and means to acquire land, God gave me a vision as to how to start. On the one hand it was thrilling and on the other, a shock to my system because God had me to start with NOTHING. No money. No land. No buildings. No faculty. No students—just His call in my heart to start, and to start with the same ingredient He used when He created the earth—nothing.

As we survey the University today as a living reality, I can testify that I didn't build it. God built it. I was, and am, an instrument in His hands. And I have been obedient. The only real virtue that I can claim is that I've obeyed God. I came under God's authority. I did what He told me to do.

We built it, starting from nothing. Therefore, God can truly say, "This is My university and not any man's." Today it is an accomplished fact—with over 1,800 full-time students, and in the evening division 950 part-time students from the greater Tulsa area. And it is under God's authority; it's built on the Holy Spirit as God said.

This entire worldwide ministry of evangelism is built and established under God's authority. I'm the first to say that God's authority is above all authority. His power above all power. And I KNOW what great faith feels like. Great faith is recognizing God's authority and power. A knowing comes into your heart that God is above all and can do everything. You know that you know, that you know, that you know!

Today there are 500 acres of land, 15 major buildings fully equipped, all costing in excess of $55 million. And again we are starting two more new buildings, as usual with no money in hand but with hearts full of Seed-Faith, the kind of stuff we've found God multiplies and builds from.

This may sound easy—I know a lot of people come by and after they see it, think it's some kind of magic that put it together. A reporter drove by and said, "It looks like somebody PLANTED a university." On the other hand, some think it is due to the ability or charisma of one man. But I know it all goes back to the 3 KEYS, combined with a divine calling to do it—hard work, and enthusiastically expecting our God to multiply the seed sown.

I want to give you an example of how the biggest building on the campus, comprising 250,000 square feet, ORU's Mabee Center (for special events), was started with the smallest seed.

HERE'S THE STORY:

Nearly 3 years ago I was present, along with other members of the administration, at the meeting of the Executive Committee of the ORU Board of Regents when we were trying to decide whether or not to build this new building.

Every person sitting there seemingly could think of nothing but the nation's economy. To start a $5½-million facility (which grew to $11 million) at that time seemed completely illogical. There were no funds, as usual, with which to start another building, and none seemed forthcoming. When asked to tell how I felt in my heart, I stood up with a feeling of impatience toward man's point of view and a determination to obey the voice of God. Not once did I raise my voice, but all of us felt the Spirit moving in that place. As I talked I thought about you, our partner, and how I knew you would like to have been there to hear what I said. I want to share a high moment in that meeting by taking you behind the scenes. Here from the minutes of the board meeting is the gist of that talk. I think you will find something that will help you get more of your needs met.

Here's what I said, the words coming up out of my inner being: "We know that many people are discouraged by the present economic conditions in the nation, but we don't live by that law. We go by our deep feelings—of feeling that God wants us to do something. And then we take action. Every building on this campus was started at a time when we had no money. (I could see heads nodding that it was so.)

"I believe this new building is in the divine plan of things for ORU for its nationwide witness. Also, it is in harmony with the *rhythm of faith and success* that we have developed over the years. This means that periodically you have to move up with a powerful new idea or program. If you don't, you come sliding to a stop. You become negative and find yourself going backward and down, and you find you have joined the rest of the people in this nation who are saying, 'This is a bad time and you can't do it.'

"I realize we don't have the money. But I believe we should commit ourselves and start moving dirt now.

"One of the regents spoke up, 'What if the funds don't come in?'"

I said, "I'd rather see us start and fail than not start moving dirt. I believe...

IF WE LOOK TO GOD AS THE SOURCE OF OUR TOTAL SUPPLY, THE MONEY WILL BE PROVIDED AND WE WILL BUILD THE BUILDING."

Then I paused, looked around, and said quietly, "Brethren, I think this is a special moment. I am saying, don't break the rhythm of faith and success we've had. It is time for ORU to advance. This will keep our rhythm going. I would fear breaking the rhythm more than I would fear launching out into the unknown. Also, let me say one more thing: I am in tune with God, with this whole ministry of world evangelism—of which ORU is a vital part—and I know that every time we have felt something deeply, and started, suddenly we found God moving in with a miracle.

"If we get afraid, then we are dead. But if we have faith—if we've been practicing the rhythm of faith—we have the assurance that comes with infinite faith. It gives us the creativity and the fearlessness to move forward with God."

69

At this point Chairman Lee Braxton asked for comments.

Regent Jack Shaw said, "The best way to get this project built is to start like we have started all the other projects, and move on by faith."

Regent Gary LaGere said, "If ORU can move forward with this project 'on faith' it will awaken people and serve as an inspiration to the country."

Vice-chairman Bob Zoppelt said, "I am excited about this project and what it can do for ORU and the country. I think there are enough people throughout this ministry who will support it. People in all walks of life are interested in sending their children to ORU because of its founding principles."

Regent Clarence Glasgow said, "YOU CAN'T GET ANYTHING DONE WITHOUT GOING AHEAD BY FAITH. If you don't go forward, you die. Let's start it now."

Regent Lamar Johnston said, "Oral Roberts is reaching more people than ever before and they are becoming aware of how ORU can help their children. But that's not all. We've got to do what God tells us to do. IT'S OUR BUSINESS TO OBEY AND GOD'S TO SUPPLY THE NEEDS."

Regent Otis Winters said, "I like President Roberts' idea on the rhythm of faith. It has begun to work in my life, and I believe we should apply it now while we're wrestling to make a decision to build this new building."

My dear wife Evelyn said, "I've found through the years of living with Oral that when he really feels something deeply he needs room to move. I agree that we must have the new building. But I agree there's something even more important, and it's that we don't break our rhythm. That we just move and then we'll see that God will use this to inspire many of our friends to move forward in faith to get more of their needs met."

By this time everybody was broken up, and when it was time to pray we were ready. You could feel the Holy Spirit moving through the room. Later we voted unanimously to start moving dirt and to trust God to see us through.

After prayer I suggested that each one present remember the second miracle key of Seed-Faith: Seed for your miracle by giving first. I suggested each one contribute one or two small bills as a little seed and think of it as the "loaves and fishes" given to Jesus by the little boy, which loaves and fishes Jesus took and multiplied to feed some 5,000 people.

Everybody in that room opened his billfold and laid something on the table, the smallest gift being $2 and the largest $100. The total amount was only $232. But to us, it was the little seed that God could start working with. It was agreed to deposit this first *"seed"* in a special account. And as we broke ground and started the new building, we would watch and see what God would do to multiply the seed we put in that day to meet what we thought would be

(Continued on page 86)

ORU's entrance—the Avenue of Flags

The heartbeat of ORU—the Prayer Tower

ORU's beautiful Mabee Center

Partners' Building and Drama Building—a twofold facility

The John D. Messick Learning Resources Center, named in honor of the renowned dean of academic affairs

Left, women's highrise dorm; center, Student Center; right, men's highrise dorm

Newly completed highrise dorms for men and women—the building in the center connects these two facilities

Aerial view of most of the campus of Oral Roberts University

ORU student body and faculty 1972-73

The Oral Roberts Association offices

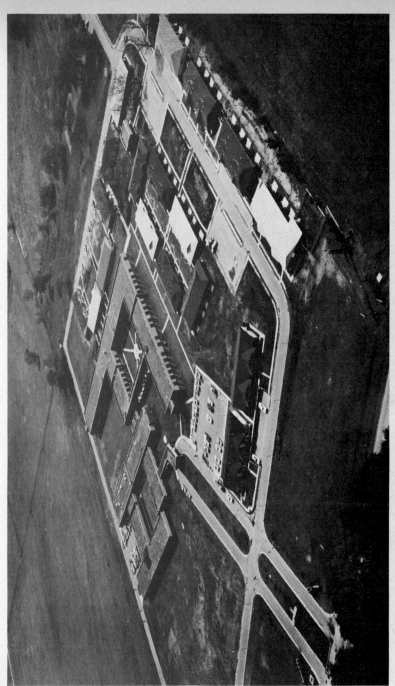

Aerial view of ORU's University Village—a retirement center for senior citizens, adjacent to the campus

At Madison Square Garden—the National Invitation Tournament—1972

ORU's Mabee Center filled as our beloved friend Billy Graham helped dedicate it. Billy graciously said, "I have preached in some of the most magnificent auditoriums all over the world, from the Nippon Budokan Hall in Tokyo to Madison Square Garden in New York, and this—the Mabee Center—is the most beautiful auditorium I think I've ever spoken in. And I think you ought to be proud of it."

the $5½-million need for the building, which we soon realized had to be much larger than we first planned.

Now the new $11-million Mabee Center is completed and it's a beauty. Over 500,000 people will be served by it the very first year! The spectacular thing to us is that when we completed it, it was more than half paid for and a very favorable loan was received for the balance. We call it our miracle building. And we feel it is no accident that the very first public meeting was conducted by our dear friend Billy Graham, with the building filled and hundreds indicating their need of Christ.

THE TITANS BASKETBALL TEAM IS ANOTHER MIRACLE

In its first year (1971-72) as a full-fledged member of the National Collegiate Athletic Association, the Titans (our basketball team) set a record scoring average of 105.1, and a rebounding average of 60.2, making us the highest scoring and rebounding team in the NCAA in '72. Richard Fuqua was second in the national scoring race, with a 35.9 average, and our team was invited to participate in the National Invitation Tournament in Madison Square Garden in New York. In the first round we beat the Missouri Valley co-champion, Memphis State, 94-74.

ACCREDITATION—ANOTHER MIRACLE

In 6 short years—another miracle in itself—Oral Roberts University received full accreditation by the North Central Association of Colleges and Secondary Schools—a fact almost unheard of in academic circles. We have a highly qualified faculty and our graduates are already making their mark across the United States. A friend said:

"Oral, you live on the brink of disaster, on the verge of a miracle."

He's right. So I believe if any man is qualified to talk about miracles out of his experiences, I am. And not just

When we received the news of our regional accreditation, I announced it in chapel. I couldn't keep the tears back. That's my darling wife Evelyn to my left—rejoicing for this, another miracle in the NOW.

in building buildings or establishing a university. I've dealt with millions of people—I've been in the arena of human needs. I've walked among people whose only hope was a miracle. I've been there when miracles happened and I've been there when they didn't. I've had great success and great failures and I AM TOTALLY CONVINCED THAT WE CAN LIVE ON THE FRONTIER OF MIRACLES IN THE NOW!

A MIRACLE IS NOT SOMETHING FOR NOTHING

People talk about a miracle as though it were magic, or some gimmick. A miracle comes from God, your Source. From the *seed* you put in. The opening up of yourself. The giving of your love—love that touches your soul, time, compassion, concern—yes, even money. *But the money has to represent something in your heart or it is not a real gift to God.* The giving of money is a by-product of love in your heart. So is anything else you give.

Not long ago a young couple stood before me and really laid out their problems. He said:

"I've lost my job—we are just sick over it. We've used up our savings—I've tried to get another job and it looks like all the doors are barred."

Then she spoke up:

"There's something else. Our marriage has been in trouble for about 3 years. One of our children is very sick—and neither of us somehow feel so well anymore..."

I SENSED THAT THEY WANTED ME TO PRAY A LITTLE SHORT PRAYER SO THEY COULD HAVE A MIRACLE FOR EVERY PART OF THEIR LIFE. "There's no way!" I said.

This was a shock!

He said, "Well, what shall we do?"

"First, take your Bible and start reading it. Then I suggest you read my book, MIRACLE OF SEED-FAITH. Then write me what you learn. Then I'll write back and you will see what to do. You will see the problem is within yourself, also God's answer. You will see the key issue is: WHO IS THE SOURCE OF YOUR SUPPLY? It isn't Oral Roberts. It isn't anybody else. It isn't a particular job. GOD IS YOUR SOURCE OF TOTAL SUPPLY.

I'm corresponding with these people now and we are beginning to see victory. He's gotten a job. Their marriage is not perfect but it's moving in the right direction as they learn to give first to each other. And in the last letter I received, the woman said:

"WE ARE ON THE VERGE OF A NEW LIFE!"

MIRACLES COME WHEN YOU MAKE GOD YOUR SOURCE AND PUT YOUR FAITH TO WORK; THAT IS, SEED FOR A MIRACLE (Key No. 2).

"Whatsoever a man soweth, that shall he also reap" (Galatians 6:7). We cannot reap that which we have not sown. We must sow the seed. This verse in Galatians 6:7 is often quoted in a negative sense. Yet it contains the secret of how to get your needs met. It tells you that you are capable of sowing that which is good, and from the good you sow, God will multiply and bring back to you a return in the form of your need.

Many dear Christians give and never expect God to give anything back. They have been taught that giving is an obligation . . . their Christian duty. Thus, they have developed a theological false modesty that violates every principle of life. <u>They put a seed in the ground and expect a harvest, but they give to God and expect nothing in return!</u> This is totally unscriptural.

But when they learn to give as a seed they sow, it often brings a transformation of their entire lives. Recently a partner from Georgia wrote me and said:

Dear Brother Roberts:

Two years ago, when I began trying to practice the 3 KEYS of Seed-Faith, I was at the end of my rope. My marriage was on the rocks. My beautiful 16-year-old daughter was rebellious and running with the wrong crowd. And I was at the point of a complete nervous collapse.

It's true that I had been giving faithfully to God's work before this but I had never expected anything from God in return. But from the Miracle of Seed-Faith book I learned that every time I give

*anything, I give it as a seed I plant and begin
to expect miracles to meet my needs.*

*Since that time God has given us so many
miracles in our family. God restored my marriage.
Today my husband and I are closer than ever. And
my daughter is now a lovely Christian. She's in
church every Sunday, singing in the choir and
going with a fine boy. She's as happy as can be.*

*We know that Seed-Faith living has put us in
God's will for our lives because His goodness has
become a large part of our family's life together.*

Sincerely,

Mr. and Mrs. F.S.M.

O O O

Jesus said, "Ask, and it shall be given you; seek and ye shall find; knock, and it shall be opened unto you" (Luke 11:9).

The finders are the seekers,
    door-openers are the knockers,
        and receivers are those who first give, then
            EXPECT when they ask.

Many people live on the verge of miracles because they have made God the Source of their Total Supply; they are seeding for a miracle by giving of themselves, but too often they stop there. <u>You must not stop with the first 2 Keys.</u> When you do your part and release your faith, God will send the miracle. The New Testament puts it this way, "Surely blessing I will bless thee, and multiplying I will multiply thee" (Hebrews 6:14). This is why you must use the third key and expect a miracle—so you will recognize it when God sends it and reach forth and receive it from

90

His hand. Otherwise, it may pass you by.

Nearly every day letters come to us from people who have grasped the exciting realization that we can experience miracles in the NOW of our lives. I was especially impressed by what our partners, Mr. and Mrs. Willis Bussart, wrote:

> Dear Brother Roberts:
>
> We turned the TV on one Sunday morning and heard you say:
>
> "EXPECT A MIRACLE"
>
> with positiveness and sincerity. You captured our attention. We'd been having real financial troubles--we had just begun to climb out of debt. We both had secured jobs and even had managed to

Mr. and Mrs. Willis Bussart

91

save $200 when the bottom dropped out. My wife underwent emergency surgery. She came through well but was told that she couldn't work for at least 6 months. The day I brought her home from the hospital, I lost my job. Talk about being scared--we were terrified.

It was the middle of winter. Snow was on the ground and jobs were hard to find--especially when you are over forty and have a history of ill health. I tramped the streets day and night looking for work. Our meager savings evaporated and a large hospital bill stared us in the face.

We had heard you talk about Seed-Faith but somehow the 3 KEYS had never really gotten hold of us. We were praying and we were giving...as for expecting a miracle--that seemed like a dream too good to be true.

Then your book, Miracle of Seed-Faith, arrived. We devoured it. In plain words it told us: GOD WAS NOT FAILING US--WE WERE FAILING HIM BECAUSE WE HAD NOT REALLY PUT HIM FIRST. Then and there we made a total commitment of our lives to Christ, without any reservations.

We had felt that there had been something lacking between God and us, like there was a door closed and we didn't know how to open it to receive God's blessings. In your book, we found the answer--we weren't giving first so we could receive. We were not EXPECTING God to do anything for us.

I had never read Luke 6:38 before but there it was, GIVE, AND IT SHALL BE GIVEN UNTO YOU...

We had so little money left--only $5 for groceries. My wife said:

"Willis, shall we give this as Seed-Faith? If God's going to help us then we have to seed for a miracle--we've got to give God something to work with!"

I thought, if she is willing to take this risk of faith...perhaps even go hungry...so am I.

Brother Roberts, something happened inside of us when we gave that Seed-Faith offering. There was a positiveness, a realization that God was very near us and would take care of our needs. This EXPECTING A MIRACLE in the NOW began to get down deep inside.

We began looking to God as our Source from day-to-day and bill-to-bill and EXPECTING A MIRACLE. Within a few days, God helped me to find full-time employment--the best job I'd ever had. A short time later, to our amazement, my wife's hospital bill was paid in full by a completely unexpected source. Talk about miracles! We were overwhelmed!

--Mr. and Mrs. Willis Bussart

O O O

It's just fabulous to see the way our ORU students grasp the 3 KEYS of Seed-Faith and the miracles God brings into their lives as they practice them. I want to share with you just a few of their testimonies:

HERE IS JOYCE LAMPKIN'S STORY AS SHE TOLD IT RECENTLY IN AN EVENING CHAPEL SERVICE:

"About a couple of years ago I thought, I really have made it. I'm going to Oral Roberts University. I make

Joyce tells her story on a half-hour telecast

good grades—I'm in the World Action Singers—and I have a witness for the Lord. I was just excited about it all when—zap! I landed in the hospital. Within a month they were telling me things about being incurable and saying:

'Kids with what you have don't live very long.'

"I said, 'Oh, Lord! Not me! It was *Job* You messed with. Not me. My name is Joyce.' I said, 'Lord, I've got a witness. I've got people to help. Lord, what are You doing? You really have messed up this time!'

"Yet it was me—in the hospital.

I couldn't talk.

I couldn't hear.

My heart was swollen.

You name it, I had it.

94

Then I thought, I'm going to watch President Roberts on the TV Sunday. I will listen to his sermon and when he says, 'I want you to pray with me,' I'm going to pray, too. I'm going to count one, two, three and say, 'Now, God, do Your stuff.' And I thought I would jump right out of that hospital bed and go home. This is the truth—this is the way I *thought* it would happen.

"So Sunday morning came. President Roberts comes on and he talks a little bit about giving. I didn't want to listen to that. He talked a little bit about loving and I didn't want to hear that. I thought, don't tell me all this other stuff. I just want to get well.

"Finally, President Roberts gets to the prayer. And I go, 'Yes, Lord, one, two, three'—

—but I'm *still* lying in bed!

I've still got a temperature.

I'm not moving.

"Then I said, 'You didn't make it that time, Joyce.' So I had to get still and think about what President Roberts had talked about. He talked about seeding for a miracle by *giving* first. And I said, 'Well, Lord, I can't give. I'm lying up here in a hospital. My mission field is out there. What can I do?'

"Well, I got it socked to me there in the hospital. From then on I got the most ding-a-ling roommates and the clumsiest nurses you have ever seen in your life. And I said, 'Lord, this is not my ministry.' But you know what??

I FOUND THAT JOYCE LAMPKIN, WHO KNEW SO MUCH ABOUT GIVING AND LOVING, DIDN'T KNOW ANYTHING!

"I had a lot to learn. I had to learn to love that roommate that talked all day long. I had to learn to love that nurse who was just a little bit late, or the big one who turned you over and you weren't ready to go. I even had to learn to love my little brother who can be very aggravating. BUT IT WAS NOT UNTIL I LEARNED TO GIVE THAT MY GOOD LORD GAVE BACK TO ME! AND DO YOU KNOW WHAT HE GAVE ME? HE GAVE ME LIFE!—not just an ordinary life—I don't have to tolerate midsemester slump. I don't have to be depressed. I don't have to live a life of loneliness—

"HE GAVE ME THAT ABUNDANT LIFE!"

"Today I'm praising the Lord for my healing. But it was not until I gave from where I was, from my want, that I received my healing from God.

"You give of yourself and you'll be healed—not only of physical problems but you'll receive healing for a crippled life, a crippled heart, a crippled relationship. THIS IS WHAT HEALING IS—HEALING FOR THE WHOLE MAN. And believe me, when I sing about 'A Life Worth Living,' I can sing it from the bottom of my soul because I'm not going to die—I'm going to live on." (Joyce returned to ORU and graduated in the Class of '72.)

□ □
□ □

"I'VE LEARNED TO GIVE WHEN THE LORD SAYS, 'GIVE!' "

Gail Letterle is attending ORU as a result of a healing he received many years ago in one of our crusades.

Gail was only 4 years old when he became sick with Hodgkin's disease. He was given 6 months to live. This crisis brought Gail's parents to the Lord and they came to the conclusion that their only hope for Gail was to turn to their Source and ask God to heal him.

When it was known that a crusade was to be held within a thousand miles of their home, they determined to take

Gail. By this time, he was weak and not able to run and play. His fingernails and toenails were turning soft and sluffing off because of the disease.

His parents detected a noticeable change after he received healing prayer in the crusade and he immediately began to get stronger.

Gail Letterle

When he was taken for a checkup a week later the doctor was amazed. Six months passed and he had progressed to the point of being a healthy little boy. The doctor called him his "miracle boy."

Years passed and Gail became a rebellious teen-ager, attending church only because he was forced. As a freshman in high school, he became involved with drugs—he knew God existed but did not have a personal relationship with Christ. Finally, some of his friends on dope were busted and this caused Gail to reexamine his life. He returned to church and accepted Christ as Savior but he still did not completely commit his life to God. When it came time for college his parents immediately thought, ORU. With very little enthusiasm, Gail attended a *youth seminar* on campus. But he liked what he saw and decided to enroll for the fall

97

semester. Recently he told me:

"When I got here I felt uneasy—like how could little old sinful me pray with all these super Christians around. I almost turned my back on God again, but about halfway through the semester I asked God to really take control of my life, and I found Jesus more real than ever before. On the ORU campus and in chapel I'd heard plenty about Seed-Faith living so I thought, WHY NOT GIVE IT A TRY?

"So I began practicing the 3 KEYS of Seed-Faith. One day the Lord impressed me to give a certain amount of money as a Seed-Faith offering. If I did, it would leave me only $2 to last 2 weeks. I wasn't sure I'd heard the Lord right. But still I felt I should give. So I did. And within 3 days the Lord returned the amount I'd given, plus more! I have learned to give when the Lord says, 'Give,' and my needs have been supplied.

"I was headed in the right direction, toward God, when I came to ORU, but here I've taken a big step toward CHRISTIAN MATURITY. I found out what the Lord COULD do, if I'd allow Him to, if I'd delight myself in Him and acknowledge that He is the Source of my Total Supply."

O O O

"WHEN EVERYTHING ELSE FAILED, GOD WAS THERE"

Sometimes the students' miracles happen in a roundabout way—like EDITH TAMSUZA, for instance—she is from Africa. Edith first read about ORU in the ABUNDANT LIFE magazine. Here's the way it happened:

Edith Tamsuza

Edith is one of 11 children. So she knew GOD would have to be her SOURCE—the Source of her Total Supply—if she could ever come to ORU. So she began to fast and pray. Through this, God just dropped a great chunk of FAITH into her heart that a way would be made—the kind of faith that makes you KNOW THAT YOU KNOW, THAT YOU *KNOW*.

The time came to go and Edith started packing, still without visible means of financial support.

... THEN MIRACLES STARTED HAPPENING

... a wardrobe of clothes was given to her—and then—

... she received a scholarship to another school in the States!

Edith was not disturbed. She figured this was God's way of at least getting her to the United States.

Edith had been in the States only about a year when she learned that the school she was attending was not fully accredited. Therefore, she had to find another school or return to Africa.

Only recently Edith shared with me how God worked it out. She said:

"What was I to do? There was no one in this country who could help me. Then I remembered from reading your story, Brother Roberts, how God had worked in *your* life. WHEN EVERYTHING ELSE FAILED—GOD WAS THERE.

"With this hope I went straight to the school

99

prayer room and talked to God. I told Him all about it. And again, through a dream, God fortified my faith.

"I dreamed I was shaking hands with you, Brother Roberts, and you were saying:

'It's nice to have you here at ORU, Edith.' I still didn't know how I would get to ORU but I knew this was where I was supposed to be.

"I applied for admission, still with no money and *still ignoring the circumstances.*

"No one gave me any encouragement. But I knew GOD WAS MY SOURCE. I will admit that things looked bad. Then just 2 weeks before I had to leave New York, some friends invited me to their home. While I was visiting with them they shared with me how God had impressed them to give me a certain amount of money. To my heart's delight, IT WAS THE EXACT AMOUNT NEEDED FOR MY FARE TO TULSA, OKLA-HOMA, AND MY TUITION FOR THE FIRST SEMESTER AT ORU. GOD HAD ANSWERED MY PRAYER!

"After a lot of prayer and hard work, I completed the requirements for a double major in theology and sociology at ORU.

"Now I am in graduate school and planning to return to my native country, Uganda, to offer my people spiritual and physical help. I want to help someone as I have been helped. I know that by placing complete faith in God and looking to Him as my Source, He will help me do this . . . and I can expect miracles always."

O O O

A miracle is not something for nothing—you must seed for your miracle, you must give _first_, before you can expect to receive.

SOLOMON, the wisest man who ever lived, said, CAST THY BREAD UPON THE WATERS: FOR THOU SHALT FIND IT AFTER MANY DAYS (Ecclesiastes 11:1).

Jesus put it this way:

"GIVE, AND IT SHALL BE GIVEN UNTO YOU" (Luke 6:38).

The Apostle Paul said, "GOD WHO GIVES SEED TO THE SOWER MULTIPLIES THE SEED SOWN" (2 Corinthians 9:10).

CASTING YOUR BREAD UPON THE WATERS IS GIVING. It is putting the seed of faith in _first. Giving is sowing in joy._ Giving is opening up your inner self and following Jesus in the now.

YOUR BREAD means your existence, your money, your time, your talent, your love, your faith, your life, your very being. And when you give yourself, always give it as unto the Lord. In other words, although your giving may be to some person, or group, you're really giving it to God your Source. What you give represents you—your heart, your love, your concern. You may give an offering of money. You may give time and concern. You may pray for someone. Or you may give something else. Or it may be a combination or part or all of these by-products of your heart. Whatever you give, it's an act of your love and faith. It is a seed sown.

ON THE WATERS. In the Bible "waters" often stands for troubled humanity. Read Revelation 13:1 about the sea, the waters, speaking of the mass of troubled humanity . . .

AND REMEMBER THIS ABOUT CASTING YOUR BREAD
UPON THE WATERS:

First, God says you will find it after many days. You shall find it.

When you cast your bread on the water, you may feel like it's gone. You may say, "I put it in and nobody cares, nobody thanks me." But the Bible says, "You SHALL find it." God will multiply it and return it. Maybe in a few days, a week—He will. But He may wait a longer time. It may be many days. But IT SHALL RETURN to you after many days. It shall return!!! This is the promise of God.

Second, the wave you cast your bread upon may not be the wave God will return it on. It may be another wave.

What this means to you is, God will return your giving— through your giving you will receive from God—BUT (and this is important to you) GOD WILL RETURN IT IN HIS OWN WAY AND AT HIS OWN TIME. I call this God's supply from an unexpected instrumentality. From someone you didn't expect would help you, or in a way you hadn't thought about. The fact is that most of the important returns from casting my bread on the water came in almost totally unexpected ways or times or from those I least expected from. But always I knew my Source, the Lord, did it! It is He I look to, not those other ways or times or people. Although I am grateful for these instruments, I give the glory to God.

I don't think God wants you to always keep trying to figure the way He's going to return your giving. He doesn't want you to dictate to Him how it should be done, or when. God is so much wiser than you are.

To make miracles happen in your life, begin today to

practice the 3 KEYS.

(1) Start making God the Source of your Total Supply.

(2) Start seeding for a miracle by giving first and

(3) Then start looking to God, and expect a miracle. Look for it. Expect it. For the miracle will come.

REMEMBER, SEEDING FOR A MIRACLE IS GIVING GOD SOMETHING TO WORK WITH. !!

NOTES

6 YES! YOU CAN PRAY FOR ALL KINDS OF MIRACLES

I WROTE THIS CHAPTER BY HAND on a yellow pad high up in a jet plane that was taking me to a guest appearance on the Dinah Shore TV Show in Hollywood, and then to another taping session of our national TV program. I was thinking of what I see when I look into the TV camera. I see a person, a person with a need. I reach out to him with my heart and hands and suddenly I feel God is there with His healing power.

I FEEL IT! I FEEL IT ALL OVER ME, ALL THROUGH ME! THE DISTANCE HAS BEEN CLOSED. THE PERSON, I BELIEVE, FEELS IT TOO

Someone asks, "How can this closeness be? You're just a man, the camera is only a mechanical instrument, and the TV set in the person's home is also a mechanical thing." By faith, that's how I feel it is. It's this faith that brings God on the scene right into each person's life. People constantly write me and tell me that during our telecasts they feel God's presence like electricity going through them, and how tears often fill their eyes as I share Jesus THE MAN, THE SON OF GOD, with them. I feel this same JESUS CLOSENESS. It just seems to burst within me, and I feel

105

like I'm reaching out across the miles and Jesus is extending His hands through mine.

When I boarded the plane I felt Jesus. High up in the clouds I felt so close—oooh, so close! Very recently God has been His usual wonderful self in revealing His Word to me, in giving me that deep feeling of compassion for people, and in touching every part of my being with the Holy Spirit. Never have I felt my faith so HIGH. I'm bubbling over.

Christ has been waking me in the night hours, pouring His words into me. Those words have been ringing in my heart. Now, for the first time, I'm writing them down. He has been saying to me, and telling me to say to you:

TURN LOOSE! TURN LOOSE!
PRAY FOR ALL KINDS OF MIRACLES!

It's terrific when God speaks like this to me. It makes my heart pound. When I feel Him like I do now, I can tell you in all confidence that God is in the Now! He is close to you and loves you and wants to heal you and supply all your needs.

I am reminded of a man who told his family, "That Oral Roberts is just a phony; don't write to him, he can't help you. All that stuff about God being in the now—that's just words. God doesn't come into your life like that; why would He want to anyhow?"

Then one day I got a letter from him! Yes. From him! —a letter full of skepticism, yet with almost a little boy's wistful hope that *maybe* God does work in people's lives in the now. I answered and thanked him for his letter, and said I was praying for him. Back came another letter. He had a need, he said, a problem he couldn't get an answer for. And despite honest doubts, he had thought of Oral Roberts.

My reply to his first letter had given him the feeling that God does care, even for him.

The need he mentioned flooded me with memories of the need I had when I first began to realize only God could help me. Tuberculosis, stuttering, loneliness, and alienation. I had come to the end of my way. And I remembered how Jesus had come to me at the point of my need and given me healing—a healing of the whole man.

I had a good time answering this man, giving him the 3 KEYS, telling him how to make God the Source of his Total Supply, how to seed for a miracle by giving first, and then to EXPECT A MIRACLE from the Lord in the NOW. I really laid Jesus on him through the 3 KEYS. Today he is a Seed-Faith partner with me. He is alive in Jesus and sharing Jesus with his friends. He recently wrote and asked me to send a dozen copies of my book, MIRACLE OF SEED-FAITH, which I did, and he is giving them to people who have a need.

I am also reminded of Mrs. Chris Houtwed. She was healed when she turned loose of her old ideas of God and began to pray for miracles. Later she wrote me:

Chris Houtwed

 Dear Brother Roberts:
I was suffering from arthritis and had been told I would just have to learn to live with it-- there was no cure. Each morning I would think, How am I going to make it through this day? I was so depressed--I felt there was nothing to live for.

107

Then one morning, while I was watching your telecast, you said:

"WHATEVER YOUR NEED IS TODAY, LOOK
FOR GOD THERE, FOR GOD COMES TO US
AT THE POINT OF OUR GREATEST NEED.
GOD IS IN THE NOW. HE LOVES YOU;
HE WANTS YOU TO BE A WHOLE PERSON--
SPIRITUALLY, PHYSICALLY, AND MENTALLY.
BELIEVE AND BE HEALED."

I thought, what a wonderful thing if this means that God includes my great need of healing in His care for me. I couldn't quite understand how this could happen to me but as you prayed, I prayed too--in my own way. When the program was over, I got up and I felt wonderful--a load had been lifted. FOR THE FIRST TIME IN YEARS I FELT GOOD! I HAD BEEN INSTANTLY HEALED! I've not needed any treatments on my back since.

My healing and practicing the 3 KEYS of Seed-Faith have brought me into a powerful new awareness of God and His love. Before this, I knew God was alive and real, but He was off in the distance somewhere--out on the west 40. (Yes, she is a farmer's wife.) God meant little in my life--I didn't know that I could look to Him as the Source of Supply for all my needs.

I'm learning to seed for a miracle and then look for God to touch my life where it needs Him most. Now, I have miracles every day--at least they are miracles to me because I _look_ for them and expect them.

-Mrs. Chris Houtwed

108

Listen, it's the most powerful moment in your life when you have a need, when you understand there is no human supply for it. Why? Because through the 3 KEYS you start thinking about Jesus coming to you in the form of that need. This is how you can get tuned in—tuned in to Jesus, as a Person, who sat where you sit, who felt what you feel, and is there with you in the moment you need Him most. This is how you can know in the innermost part of your being that Jesus is a Person and He is in the NOW and He is concerned about you!

At this point, Jesus' words in John 10:10 flashed into my mind, "I am come that they might have life, and that they might have it more abundantly."

Flying along on the big jet I said to Jesus, "The ABUNDANT LIFE that You came to give us—is this what You mean when You say, 'TURN LOOSE! TURN LOOSE! PRAY FOR ALL KINDS OF MIRACLES?' Is this what you mean, Jesus?"

Clearly, His answer was:

"All life is from Me, your life at birth, your natural human life, but there is a more abundant life. This is miracle life, only by many miracles can you have it."

I said, "Jesus, this means then that there is a supernatural life in the now for each of us?"

"Yes."

"How can I interpret this to people?"

"Listen, and I will tell you."

I'll tell you, by this time I was feeling all tingly inside, goose bumps were on goose bumps. I began to write as fast as I could, and here is His message to you:

FIRST, JESUS WANTS YOU TO TURN LOOSE ALL YOUR THOUGHTS ABOUT THE LIMITATIONS OF YOUR NATURAL LIFE . . . AND START THINKING ABOUT

109

THAT SUPERNATURAL LIFE, THAT MORE ABUNDANT LIFE, FOR SOUL, SPIRIT, AND BODY . . . FOR YOUR WHOLE PERSON

In interpreting this to you, I get the distinct impression that Jesus feels you are not paying enough attention to your body. He tells me to remind you of the Scriptures:

> Your body is the temple of the Holy Spirit (1 Corinthians 6:19).

> Present your bodies a living sacrifice, holy, acceptable unto God, which is your reasonable service (Romans 12:1).

He says your body is not made for sickness but for health. You are not to abuse and desecrate the house He lives in—your body—with alcohol, cigarettes, immorality, fighting, overeating, or even physical ease, or with negative thoughts.

He says, with all your absorption of medical help, to remember the Bible says, "I am the Lord . . . that healeth thee."

Medicine, exercise, wholesome food—all these things are great instruments but they are not sufficient within themselves. God alone is SOURCE for your physical well-being. (Remember . . . Key No. 1: GOD is the SOURCE of your Total Supply.) He says to remind you that "the prayer of faith shall save the sick [person], and the Lord shall raise him up" (James 5:15).

Again, I am reminded of a dear friend who went to the dentist with an abscessed tooth. The dentist just frankly said, "I don't see any way to save this tooth," and the man said, "Are you saying to me that I may lose this tooth?"

"Well, it looks like it."

"Can you do no more?"

"As far as I know, this is all that can be done."

"OK," he said, "I'll let you know." In a couple of days my friend went back to the dentist and had his tooth examined. The dentist was overwhelmed and said, "This tooth is OK. Did you go to another dentist?"

"No, I didn't."

"Are you sure?"

"Yes."

"Well, what did you do?"

"Well, Doctor, when you said that you could do no more, that's when I had faith. I somehow couldn't believe God would heal my tooth as long as I thought He would use you—use medicine. But when I found that you couldn't do it, somehow I got my mind back on my Source. During the night, something happened. This morning I awakened and the pain was gone, the swelling was gone, my tooth felt fine."

The doctor said, "Well, I can assure you the tooth is fine now."

NOW IT'S VERY IMPORTANT TO REALIZE THAT WHETHER IT'S A DOCTOR, OR IT'S PRAYER, OR IT'S BOTH, THE SOURCE OF ALL HEALING IS GOD. THE SOURCE IS GOD.

For some reason some people who believe in healing through prayer, turn off doctors; on the other hand, some of those who have great faith in doctors may tune out prayer. With them it's an either/or proposition. But this is not scriptural. Our Lord said, *They that are sick need a physician* (Mark 2:17). So I accept prayer. I accept medicine, and I do it gladly and reverently.

Some time ago I became very ill with a kidney stone. If you've ever had this experience, then you know how painful it is. Evelyn called the Prayer Tower and then asked some of our men on the staff to pray for me. She

also called our family doctor. He came and gave me a shot.
Then he said, "Oral, I've treated you medically; now I want
to pray for you." Then he reached over to me on the bed,
laid his hands on me, and began to pray. It was a simple
short prayer, but full of sincerity and faith. By that time,
I really felt that I had been ministered to. In one hour I
was OK. Now I don't know if it was because of prayer
or because of medication, or both. It doesn't matter . . . I
was well. And to be honest, I don't make demands on God.
If God wants to heal me through prayer, I accept it from
Him. *If God chooses to use a doctor as the instrument to
bring healing to me, then I accept that. Or if it's a combination of both, I gratefully accept it.*

Jesus says to pay attention to your body by treating it
as an instrument of the Lord and He will give you better
health and more strength.

SECOND, JESUS WILL PENETRATE YOUR SPIRIT WHERE
SO MANY DISEASES AND PROBLEMS ORIGINATE . . .
HE WILL GIVE YOU NEW LIFE IN THE INNER MAN

My flesh tingles as I tell you this. Your spirit is your
inner man, your real self. You live in your body and there's
constant interaction between your inner man and the outer
man. Jesus says it is absolutely imperative to see yourself
inside your body as a restless problem-centered person, who
often is part of the problem rather than a part of the
answer.

<u>You may have a problem of guilt</u>. Jesus reminds
you to study John 5:1-15 concerning the man who had
been ill 38 years, both physically and in the inner man.
Instead of giving to people first, this man had lived always
expecting people to give something to him. When he did
not receive, he gave up and lay there all those lonely years

112

eating his heart out, resenting people for getting ahead of him, and filling himself with bitterness. Jesus told him:

"Take up your bed and walk."

He is saying:

"You're filled with resentment and guilt in your inner self; this is a sin that is blocking out My healing power. Get up on the inside first; start thinking thoughts of love and showing concern for other people, and you will feel the power to walk again." The man got up and walked and was made whole. Then Jesus said to him, "Go and sin no more."

In the connection in which He told him to "Go, and sin no more," He is telling you your attitude must be changed. You can change it only by using your will to get up in the innner man and to reenter the human race as a loving, giving, seed-sowing human being. Today, this moment, start realizing you are an important person to God, your body is important, your spirit has the God-given power to reject all these negative forces. You can TURN LOOSE AND BELIEVE FOR ALL KINDS OF MIRACLES. You can take up your "bed" and walk again.

I'm thinking of another plane I heard about which lost two of its four motors and the power to maintain altitude. First, they dumped the excess gasoline. Next, they ordered the passengers to throw their luggage overboard. In this way the plane made it safely to the nearest airport, and every life was saved. The passengers said to each other, "At first I didn't want to give up my luggage but what's so important about my suitcase compared to my life?"

Jesus asks you, "Are you carrying a load that is too much for the engines of your mind, spirit, and body?" Jesus is probing your soul for guilt. He's asking you about forgiving other people, about receiving forgiveness for yourself.

113

If you carry around a hateful spirit, it will ultimately sink you; it will bring you down in despair and defeat.

Jesus says, don't hang on to your resentment and guilt— *turn loose!* Get a touch of that supernatural life. Be FREE, FREE in Jesus.

THIRD, JESUS TELLS ME TO TELL YOU HE DEMANDS THAT YOU WANT TO BE WELL

I hear it ringing in my soul, "Want to be well! Desire your problems to be solved, your needs to be met. I have come to GIVE YOU more abundant life." It's hard to imagine someone NOT WANTING to be well. Yet it happens. I remember the experience of one of our dear partners.

Ruth Crum was in the hospital being treated for a complete nervous breakdown and hypoglycemia (the opposite of sugar diabetes). One Easter morning she turned on her radio just as I was concluding my broadcast with the healing prayer. I said, "If you want my prayer for your healing, lift your heart and pray with me." And there in the loneliness and desperation of her room, Ruth lifted her heart to her Lord.

She told me, "As I prayed I began to feel God's presence come into my being through my inner darkness just as clearly as I have ever felt anything in my life. What an Easter for me! What a resurrection!"

Shortly she was released from the hospital and returned to her family. However, although Ruth continued to improve, her mind was still troubled and her nerves frayed. Sometime later at one of our partners' meetings she asked me to pray for the complete healing of her mind.

Still later she told me, "That day, as we were driving home, I remembered the question Jesus asked the lame

114

Ruth Crum

man at the pool of Bethesda, *Wilt thou be made whole?* For I had found, just as you had pointed out, that some people don't want to 'pick up their bed.' Their illness is a form of security. I hate to admit it but this was true in my case. Because I was sick, everyone gave in to me—they treated me like a china doll and handled me with kid gloves. But then I realized that the Lord couldn't be pleased with this kind of attitude when I had asked for the healing of my mind. So I answered my own question—'Yes, I do want to be made whole. I want to care for my family, take my share of responsibility, and live a full life.' This is when I received my final release. I felt it in my spirit and I began to feel better from that moment on. Today I'm the happiest person I know."

Ruth frequently attends seminars on the ORU campus. Every time I see her, the brightness of her countenance gives me a lift.

Listen, Jesus says <u>to regain life</u>. <u>Lift up your heart.</u> <u>Start singing again</u>. Start giving again. He says to reach out your hand to someone. Pray for someone today. Get loose. <u>Get on the straight line to abundant life.</u>

FOURTH, JESUS SAYS TO PAY ATTENTION TO SEED-FAITH, AND START USING THE 3 KEYS (memorize these 3 KEYS), THEN EXPECT MANY MIRACLES, ALL KINDS OF MIRACLES

He says you can make it if you realize who your Source is . . . not man, not a thing, or things . . . but GOD HIM-

SELF. "I . . . am come . . . that you . . . might have . . . life more abundantly." The "I" is JESUS. *"My God . . . shall supply . . . all your need . . . "* God will supply all your need.

It's through making God the Source of your Total Supply, putting Him first in your wants and in your attitude, that you can TURN LOOSE AND SUCCESSFULLY PRAY FOR ALL KINDS OF MIRACLES.

But the seed has to be put in by you. You have to give God something to work with. The seed of concern and compassion, the seed of your God-given time, the seed of the money God has given you. No matter how little you think you have . . . or how you feel it's not enough . . . SOW IT OUT OF YOUR WANT, YOUR DEEPEST NEED . . . do it first . . . in joy and faith, knowing in your heart this is SEED-FAITH, this is "seeding for a miracle." Then . . . and only then . . . START EXPECTING ALL KINDS OF MIRACLES.

I am thinking now of a letter I received recently from a couple. The wife was steadily deteriorating in body and spirit; she couldn't do her housework. Then one Sunday I asked my television viewers to touch each other, to pray, and to expect a miracle. She wrote:

Dear Brother Roberts:

At first it was all so strange to us. We'd about given up. Then my husband reached for my hand and as you prayed we prayed—he for me, then I for him. We opened our eyes and looked at each other. Something tingly was going through me. I cried out! Beaming, my husband helped me stand, and I started walking. That was 2 weeks ago and I'm almost completely well again. And just to

117

*think that I could have had this before if I had
known God was interested in giving me this type
of miracle. Thank you so much for teaching us
this on your precious telecast.*

--Mrs. T. M.

What stands out in my mind is her remark, "I could
have had this before if I had known God was INTERESTED
in giving me *this kind of miracle*." Remember Jesus' words
to me and you:

TURN LOOSE! TURN LOOSE!
PRAY FOR ALL KINDS OF MIRACLES!
BIG OR SMALL, IT MAKES NO DIFFERENCE

One day, when we were taping at NBC in Burbank, one
of the camera crew said to me, "Mr. Roberts, I've licked
alcohol. For over 12 years alcohol had licked me. And it
had virtually ruined my home, my marriage, my own personal life, even my health, but I licked it. But the thing
that I can't lick is this little thing here in my hand. (And
he held up a cigarette.) The doctors have said to me:
'This is
    bad ...
        ` bad ...
            bad' ...
But really I've found it is easier to lick alcohol than it
is this little cigarette."

"Well," I said, "how did you lick alcohol?"

He looked at me and said, "For one thing, I prayed."

"How did you pray?"

"Well, I prayed for help. I tried to stop several times
myself, but I didn't have the power within me and I asked

God to give me power."

"And you lost the appetite?"

"I've lost it completely. But this little thing. Really, I'm embarrassed to ask God for such a little thing."

"Well," I said, "if it's so big that it's got you licked it's really not little, is it? And no matter what it is, if it is big in your life it's big to God. So why don't you just talk to God about the cigarette like you did the alcohol? The same God who took away the appetite for alcohol can take away the appetite for cigarettes."

"He can? I never thought about it from that angle."

I said, "In Matthew 17:20 Jesus said:

> If you have faith as a grain of mustard seed, you can say to this mountain [He was talking about a mountain of need, a mountain of problems in your life], *be thou removed and it will obey you.*

119

"Jesus tells you to have faith in Him by putting a seed in. Then you will see how God can take this little (big) mountain of cigarettes and help you tell it to be gone—to be gone forever."

He said, "Would you have a little prayer with me?"

I said, "Sure, but let's make it a two-way prayer. Let's pray for one another, like the Bible says, and then make it a Seed-Faith prayer." We did, and I went about my taping and forgot about it. But he didn't forget. During the next taping session, who did I see walking up with a big smile? You're right. Him!

"It's gone," he said simply.

Now there are all types of needs—mountains of needs—that we face, but God is concerned about each of them because He's concerned about you. He's concerned about you as a person; He's concerned about you as a family, He's concerned about every detail of your life. God loves you!

I'm just bubbling over in my spirit with joy and anticipation at the kinds of miracles you're going to receive. Expect all kinds of miracles.

O O O

REMEMBER WHAT I'VE BEEN SHARING WITH YOU.

God is in the NOW! He is close to you and loves you. He wants to heal you and supply ALL your needs (Philippians 4:19).

IT'S THE MOST POWERFUL MOMENT IN YOUR LIFE WHEN YOU HAVE A NEED, when you understand that there is no human supply for it, and you start thinking about Jesus coming to you in the form of that need. This is how you can know in the innermost part of your being that Jesus is a Person and He is in the NOW.

Jesus wants to penetrate your spirit where so many diseases and problems originate . . . He wants to give you new life in the inner man, and you want Him to do it.

Jesus demands that you WANT to be well. To *will* to be well. To *believe*.

To become part of the answer instead of part of the problem—start *seeding* for your miracle—this gives God something to work with.

PRAY FOR ALL KINDS OF MIRACLES! *BIG* OR *SMALL*, IT MAKES NO DIFFERENCE . . .

START EXPECTING

ALL KINDS OF MIRACLES

IN THE NOW

NOTES

7 HOW TO PRAY FOR YOUR HEALING AND KNOW THAT GOD WILL ANSWER

Mrs. Marie Fischer

SOME TIME AGO one of our faculty members at Oral Roberts University, Mrs. Marie Fischer, discovered that she had cancer in the advanced stages. She underwent surgery and miraculously recovered. That is, she recovered physically. In her spirit she was haunted by some research material she had read—that only one out of three people who had cancer as advanced as she did, lives. The fear of recurring cancer preyed on her mind with the appearance of every little physical symptom.

The following summer she became ill again. Her blood pressure soared far beyond a safe level; she was dizzy and continually nauseated. Her doctor was able to bring her

123

blood pressure under control but could not seem to find the cause of the nausea and dizziness. It was only a few weeks before the fall term was to begin. Later she shared with me how God came to her in her hour of need. She said:

"Fear tormented me day and night. I was so sick and seemingly nothing could be done. So I thought, *I'll try praying for my healing* . . .

"I began . . . 'Lord, I love You. You know that I've given my life to You, that it's my heart's desire to serve You, for I have served You these many years. I take care of my health. I eat the foods that are healthful for me. I do everything I am supposed to do . . . '

"On and on I went. Finally I stopped and the Lord spoke to my heart:

" 'IF YOU'D BE QUIET LONG ENOUGH WE COULD HAVE A CONVERSATION.'

"I thought, that makes sense. And the Lord seemed to say, 'Sure, Marie, you've given your life to Me. You've been saved a long time. But you haven't learned as much as I hoped you would.'

" 'What should I do?'

"And the Lord said, 'What is it that you want?'

" 'I want healing.'

"He said, 'How about planting a seed of healing for someone else who is in need of healing?'

"OF COURSE!!! It was just as though a light came on. *The 3 KEYS of Seed-Faith living had worked in other areas of my life. Why not use the 3 KEYS to bring about my healing?*

"Immediately I set about obtaining the names of people who had a need for healing: a man who was going to have brain surgery—another one who was to have heart surgery

—a child who was seriously ill. I got out of bed and I began to walk back and forth across the floor with the list in my hand.

"I asked myself, How would you feel if you were facing brain surgery? GET IN THERE! <u>FEEL</u> COMPASSION. PUT YOURSELF IN HIS SHOES. BE WITH THAT PERSON.

"And I did. I went down my list calling the name of every person and praying with real heartfelt compassion. And when I knew I had reached this point I said, 'Now, Lord, be with this person. Let him live and move and have his being in You . . . as You did for me.'

"For 3 days I prayed like this.

IT WASN'T EASY

The first 2 days I was weak and dizzy and nauseated. I had to hold on to the furniture to keep my balance. But I tried to ignore my symptoms. And the more I concentrated on these people and their needs, the less I thought of myself. Eventually I became relaxed in my praying. I really enjoyed this time of intercession. *And by the end of 3 days of praying for others, I found that I was perfectly healed.* When school opened I was refreshed, rejuvenated, and ready. And I've felt just great ever since."

BEFORE WE CAN BE HEALED WE NEED TO . . .
OPEN UP!
OPEN UP!
OPEN UP!

Receiving a miracle of healing is a struggle. It's not something that happens just like snapping your fingers.

You have to lay a foundation for it. There's a preparation
of your inner man. There's an opening up of your heart.
You have to start by doing something first.

The Bible says, *Confess your faults one to another, and
pray one for another, that ye may be healed. The effectual
fervent prayer of a righteous man availeth much* (James
5:16).

You see, HEALING is not the major problem. There
would be much more healing among us if this were true.
The great problem is us who are sick. Our resentments,
our confessions that we don't always make, our pulling
back from people rather than praying one for another, the
closing of ourselves to people and to God, refusing to open
up our hearts for fear we will look bad or somebody will
look down on us. BEFORE WE CAN BE HEALED WE
NEED TO OPEN UP . . . OPEN UP . . . OPEN UP . . .
OPEN UP!

The Bible tells us to "confess our faults," indicating
that we <u>have</u> them. It also says that the prayers of a
<u>righteous</u> man are very effective. I think there are two
extremes that we can go to:

One is feeling so unrighteous, so unworthy, that we
can't pray.

The other is to feel so righteous that we feel we don't
<u>need</u> to pray.

I think the middle course is to know in our heart that
we are moving in the direction of our Lord's life. When
we make a mistake, we confess it and ask God to forgive us.
We go to the person we've wronged and try to make it right.
(Whether he forgives us is not the main thing, it's the
action of asking for it.) This is RIGHTEOUSNESS . . .
this is moving in the direction God moves in.

Now the Lord understands that there are occasions

when you can't go to the person who has wronged you, or whom you may have wronged. The person may be dead or far removed from you. Sometimes it is best not to say anything because you might make it worse. And the Lord understands that. But there is one thing you can do and that is to open up, open up, and breathe God's love toward that person. It's a way of opening the door.

That brings up another important point—

YOU DON'T NEED TO HAVE A DAILY SEARCH-PARTY LOOKING FOR YOUR FAULTS

If you are honest before God, HE will bring to your mind the things that need confessing.

I was praying one day when I had a tremendous urge to write a letter to a man who had wronged me. The Holy Spirit was urging me to write and tell him how sorry I was and ask him to forgive me. My human reaction was:

Why should I ask HIM to forgive me? I didn't do him wrong. HE did me wrong.

But the Spirit had searched deep within my inner self and found a resentment in me because this man had done me wrong. I had carried that resentment for about 2 years but I was not really aware of it. All I know is that every time I thought about that man I got a sick feeling in the pit of my stomach.

The Holy Spirit revealed to me that was resentment. I saw my resentment was wrong, that the fact he had wronged me did not justify my resenting him. I saw that I had to love him as though he had never wronged me. Well, I've never found that easy to do. But I wrote him a letter and told him that I felt badly toward him and I wanted him to forgive me. When I mailed the letter I felt great. It never occurred to me he would even answer me. But lo and behold! he wrote me a beautiful letter and said, "I am the one who needs to apologize . . . " Today we are great friends. But even if he had not replied, I still would have felt good. I had done what the Bible says and it caused me to feel released. There was a healing of my own spirit.

We all have faults, shortcomings, failures. There are places where none of us measure up like we ought. There are days when we can sing and rejoice and feel close to God. There are other days when we feel that God is a million miles away. It's hard on those days and maybe we will say things we shouldn't say and do things we ought not to do. And our Lord says, "Accept the fact that you have faults. Accept the fact that your brothers and your sisters have faults. But just go ahead and love one another. Accept one another—warts and all!!!"

"Pray one for another, that ye may be healed" (James 5:16). The emphasis here is upon the ONE doing the praying. Now I've had the privilege of traveling throughout five continents, in scores of the major cities, into the countryside, the bush of Africa, and the packed cities of the Far East. I've dealt with people in the masses, in small groups, and face-to-face. I know from personal experience that this Scripture is possibly the most important thing that you and I can learn for our healing. Often when I pray for someone I suggest a two-way prayer —I ask him to pray for me FIRST before I begin my prayer for him. This is to help the sick person plant the seed of concern for someone else, FIRST. The Master is saying:

"You pray for someone else to be healed so that *YOU* also may be healed." He is saying:

"Put the seed in first, so I can have something from your heart to work with."

He's trying to get you and me opened up inside. Deep

128

down, each of us is inhibited. We are tense. We don't often let the real person come out. We are taught from infancy not to reveal our inner heart because people might misunderstand or betray us. They might think less of us if we are totally frank. And it's true. People are not like God. They don't know how to be merciful or how to appreciate one another properly.

But when we need healing in any area of our lives, we are dealing directly with the Healer, God. And He's saying to us, "OPEN UP! OPEN UP! Pray ye one for another that ye may be healed." It is another way of saying, GIVE, AND IT SHALL BE GIVEN UNTO YOU (Luke 6:38) — another way of Seeding for a Miracle.

A man said to me:

"Brother Roberts, what does giving have to do with my healing?"

It has everything to do with it. A closed hand, or a fist, is symbolic of anger. An open hand shows interest, concern, and compassion. Remember, in healing you're dealing with God. You're not going to get healing from God as long as you are mad or angry or living in a rage—upset about this, that, or the other. You have got to calm down and realize that obedience to God is better than sacrifice. You may go to church, but that is no substitute for obedience to God. You may listen to a fine sermon on Sunday morning, but that cannot take the place of hearing God's still small voice in your own heart. You may even give your finances, but that cannot take the place of giving yourself to God. It's important to you to give of your finances. However, for it to be a seed of faith it has to be a by-product of your heart that you are opening up to God and to others. Otherwise, it's just a piece of money. It is not a seed of faith at all.

129

IF YOU NEED HEALING . . .

1. Recognize that God is the Source of all healing whether the answer comes through medical aid, through prayer, or a combination of both.

2. Confess your faults.

3. Open up your inner man. Learn to give. Plant a seed for someone else's healing. "Pray one for another, that ye may be healed" (James 5:16).

4. Obey God. What He says to you, do it. Marie prayed for the healing of others for 3 days. God will impress you what to do.

5. EXPECT A MIRACLE! (Remember Key No. 3.)

8 WHAT TO DO WHEN THE LIGHTS GO OUT IN <u>YOUR</u> WORLD

A FARMER PUT ON HIS WEATHERVANE the words, "GOD IS LOVE." A cynical neighbor came by and said, "Is your God so fickle that He just changes with the winds?"

"No," the farmer replied, "I put 'God is love' on the weathervane, because NO MATTER WHICH WAY THE WIND BLOWS, GOD IS LOVE. HE DOESN'T CHANGE."

It's one thing to say that God is love, that God wants you to prosper and be in health, that He wishes all good for you, that He is your Source. It's quite another to trust God as your Source when grief tears you apart and

WHEN ALL THE LIGHTS
GO OUT IN YOUR WORLD.

Yet it is in the midst of such trying circumstances that many of our partners have proven the <u>ruggedness</u> of God's love and of Seed-Faith living.

O O O

Recently Ed Gish, a friend of this ministry, shared with me how learning to make God the Source of his total life brought him through unbearable grief. Here's the way he tells it:

"Bitterness and hate had eaten away at my insides until I was just a shell of a man. I blamed the doctor and God for letting our 3-year-old son die. If you have ever allowed hate to get inside you, you can understand how it can destroy your thinking, twist your mind, wither your inner man, and make you blind to reality.

"My wife Judy and I attended church regularly but we didn't really have a Source for our lives. We felt no real need. Everything was going great. God had blessed our home with a beautiful baby daughter. Then 2 years later our son was born. We felt we had a perfect little family and thanked God for it.

"Then we learned that little Jay had been born with an open spine (spinal bifida). And the doctor said his chances were mighty slim. We were brokenhearted. I went home from the hospital and prayed like I'd never prayed before. I said:

" 'God, let little Jay live and give me strength to work

Stacy, Ed, Judy, and Scott Gish

and pay all the doctor and hospital bills . . . this is all I ask . . . ' And I felt the Lord gave me the assurance that Jay would live and that I was not to worry about the financial part.

"Surgery was performed before Jay was 24 hours old. He remained in the hospital 4 weeks. I tell you I spent many nights in prayer. Finally the day came when we were told to bring Jay home. What a celebration we had. However, our joy was cut short. For in just 3 weeks his head began to swell. Examination revealed he had developed hydrocephalus. A shunt to his heart was installed, and a little bulb placed beneath his scalp had to be pumped daily.

"The struggle and burden of it all was just too much, and as the bills began to pour in I really began to question God. 'Where is the help You promised?' I wondered if He had forgotten our address, if He remembered our name . . . if He was concerned with Jay and our problems.

"I felt that Jesus was ten million miles away—that my prayers were lost in outer space. Still, I held a glimmer of hope that God was not too far and would somehow hear my plea and answer.

"It wasn't long before I began getting overtime on my job—the first time this had happened in years. This helped to relieve the financial pressures a little, but Jay continued to grow worse. Then, just before he was 3 years old, complications developed that required three more operations . . . we never brought Jay home again.

"We were brokenhearted. Life had to go on but I closed myself in with grief. I couldn't understand why God would spare our son's life at birth, only to take him 3 years later. I sat up late almost every night reading the Bible, but I didn't find any answers. My grief turned to bitterness, then to hate. My wife and I drifted away from the church, away from each other, and we neglected our daughter Stacy.

"One day Stacy's teacher called. She said, 'I didn't want to bring this up—I know you and Mrs. Gish have suffered a great loss—but I'm afraid we have a real problem with Stacy. Lately she has become rebellious, she refuses to pay attention, and her grades are getting dangerously low. I have talked with some of her other teachers and we feel she needs psychiatric help . . . '

"It was like I had been slapped in the face. How could I have been so blinded with hate that I couldn't see that we had neglected Stacy.

"About this time our church had a lay witness mission and we were asked to take a young couple into our home for the weekend. We agreed. This couple may have *thought* they came for the mission, but Judy and I know they were sent to us directly from God.

"LIFE TOOK ON MEANING ONCE AGAIN"

"Through their witness and understanding Judy and I really came back to Christ—and for the first time really came to know Him as a Person. The love of Jesus in our lives gave us strength to accept the loss of our little son. We had a Source for our lives again. And all the hate, the bitterness, and the grief just melted away and life took on meaning once again.

"In no time at all, Stacy's emotional problems were resolved without the aid of a psychiatrist. All she really needed was for Mother and Daddy to give her their love and attention again."

What do you do to overcome grief? A grief so dark, like Ed's, that turns to bitterness and then to hate. First of all, you have to accept it. We have to accept grief as a fact because there is no easy way to give up a little child or a wife or a husband or a father or a mother. It hurts. We have to accept it. We can't continue acting like it's strange; it's a fact of life. But we don't have to live with it. We can come back to the Source of our life. Remember, Ed said, "THE LOVE OF JESUS IN OUR LIVES GAVE US STRENGTH TO *ACCEPT* THE LOSS OF OUR LITTLE SON." Only GOD can heal the broken heart (Luke 4:18). So lay it before Him. Stop trying to find an answer to the endless questions of, "Why?" Turn loose! Get back to the Source of your life, your Source of Total Supply. Open your mind to a miracle of healing in your emotions and memories.

Turn outward, look around you, and become involved in the needs of others through the 3 KEYS. Give God something to work with. Ed's healing began when he realized that he had focused his life completely on his grief. He had turned away from his wife and away from his daughter. He suddenly realized that *he* wasn't the only one with a broken heart—their hearts were also broken and, worse still, his hate and bitterness—his turning his back on them—was making their grief harder to bear. So he began to give of his love and concern for them. He opened up and started giving again (Key No. 2).

"MIRACLE OF SEED-FAITH WAS LIKE A COMPASS"

Then one day Ed was visiting with his friends who had led him back to God, and Jack said, "How much are you giving to God's work, Ed?"

"Why, Jack, I'm working myself to the bone trying to get our medical bills paid—how do you expect me to give to God?"

Then he said, "I've got a book you must read." And

he reached over and handed him a copy of MIRACLE OF SEED-FAITH. This book turned Ed around. He later shared with me, "Brother Roberts, this was the most wonderful book I have ever read. God has already done a lot for me spiritually but that book was like a compass—it pointed me to a way out. For the first time I realized how to look to God as the Source of my Total Supply—not only for my spiritual needs, but also in financial matters. I saw that I could give to God first so He could have something to work with and He would take care of the rest. I stopped looking at my bills and started looking to my Source [Key No. 1]. Immediately we started giving to God in love. Our 'depth,' as you call it [pages 40 and 41 in MIRACLE OF SEED-FAITH], was small at first, but God multiplied what we gave. Again and again the company gave me overtime—in fact, all I could handle. In this, I saw the hand of God multiplying what we were giving to Him. [Key No. 2 is seeding for a miracle by giving first.]

"Today we are able to pay our bills. Also we have a new home and a new life. All this did not come easy. WE STRUGGLED—we suffered—we sometimes thought God had forgotten.

"Although the Holy Spirit had healed our grief, there were occasions when we felt that ache of emptiness—we missed little Jay so. Then we began to think, *if only we could adopt a little boy it would help so much to take the place of Jay* [Key No. 3—expecting a miracle]. We decided that we wanted to adopt a child right away. But the Lord knew best—it was well over a year before we got little Scotty. The moment we saw him we knew the Lord had chosen him for us. And we knew God's timing was right.

"We have learned, day by day, that the Lord knows what

He is doing. Had we gotten Scotty as soon as we thought we wanted him, we probably would always have been comparing him to Jay. But <u>the love of Jesus filled the vacancy Jay's death left in our lives</u>. And now Scotty is filling his own special place in our lives."

Has your life been struck by blinding grief? Do you wonder if life can ever again have any meaning? RIGHT NOW . . . in the midst of your sorrow . . . God wants to come to you and fill that emptiness with His love. He stands ready to stride into the heartbreak and impossibilities of your situation, to fill it with His life, to turn your sorrow into joy. He asks only that you give it to Him.

Approach God with your emptiness . . .

your heartbreak . . .

as a SEED-PLANTER.

Recognize that He is the Source of your healing from grief. Only *God* can mend your broken heart. Only He can help you.

Plant all your deep grief . . .

right down in the great heart of God.

Leave it there in faith. And expect the miracle of your own heart's resurrection! <u>Expect to find new life again in Christ</u>. God will fill your emptiness with the fullness of His joy.

NOTES

9 HOW TO CURE YOUR LONELINESS

THERE IS A VASTNESS in the world that we feel today. In the midst of a population explosion we suffer from this inner ache called LONELINESS. Technology has shut us off from one another; we feel alienated and alone. The pressures of modern society that keep us running pell-mell, leave little time for neighborliness, friendliness, and concern which increases our feeling of alienation.

There's a "rootlessness" among most people in our nation today. We live in a mobile society which often adds to our aloneness. It often upsets our equilibrium to go to a new place, to take a new job. Often we are forced into a new set of circumstances—perhaps through divorce, the separation war causes, or even through death—and we are left lonely. We feel uprooted. We may feel uncomfortable with the boss where we work, or a personality clash. As an employer, you may feel that your employees are not working—not doing the job—and you feel there's nothing you can do about it.

More often than not, it's hard for us to believe, in our circumstances, that God is a personal God who is concerned and who cares about us. But there is an answer, and

139

I want to share some fascinating stories to which you can relate.

Ruth Merrell, a retired schoolteacher, wrote me about the terrible loneliness in her life. After her father's death Ruth's emptiness became more acute. SHE FELT SO ALONE. In her letter I sensed an intense desire to really KNOW Christ, to find a sense of BELONGING, and to enjoy the abundant life that she had heard me discuss on the television programs and in the ABUNDANT LIFE magazine.

Here is a portion of what Ruth said in one of her letters:

Dear Brother Roberts:

For months since my father's death I have been getting sore knees from so much prayer. But all to no avail--my prayers seemed to bounce off the ceiling. I was in desperate need of spiritual help. I could no longer pull myself up by my own bootstraps.

Finally, I sensed that my first need was to believe in and feel real forgiveness from God for all my sin. A few days later your letter came. I had written you and asked prayer for healing and spiritual rebirth. Your compassion, minus any criticism; your empathy; your starting with me as I was, accomplished a turning point. I feel it was a rise in personhood (a terribly needed thing for me). I felt also a beginning in healing of anguish and of rebirth...a new being resulting from my willing commitment, plus the new touch in some way of the Holy Spirit. I was a new creature! I now feel that the great empti-

Ruth Merrell

ness within me will, in God's goodness, be filled someday, somehow by Him. But I know I shall be able to live that abundant life that I want so much.

Meanwhile, I have made a start in that direction. I have learned through reading your <u>Miracle of Seed-Faith</u> that receiving begins with giving-- giving of oneself--and this is what I have started doing. One of the things I am doing is reading <u>Miracle of Seed-Faith</u> to two elderly women who cannot see well enough to read for themselves.

141

And already ripples are going out from that in all directions, and I get triple benefit.

I know I still have a long way to go but now I, at least, know the way...

--Ruth Merrell

A few months later I received another letter from Ruth, and was she ever bubbling over! In her letter she told me how she had now received the glorious infilling with the Holy Spirit.

ΠΠΠ

Someone has said, "Hell is being alone, being away, being out of touch . . . not to understand or be understood, not to love or be loved." I think Ruth must have felt this way. But she found the answer in God.
Ruth learned for herself that . . .
Regardless of where you live . . .
Regardless of your set of circumstances . . .
Regardless of how lonely you are . . .
    you are never alone. Do you know why?
"The eternal GOD IS YOUR . . . DWELLING PLACE"
    (Deuteronomy 33:27, *The Amplified Bible*).
AND LISTEN TO THIS:
"For in him [God] we LIVE, AND MOVE, AND HAVE OUR BEING" (Acts 17:28). You've got to know and remember this: God is your dwelling place.
A story called "Marooned" tells about the astronauts on their way to the moon. And because the moon's atmosphere is poisonous, no man can breathe it and live more

142

than a few seconds. So their spacecraft was equipped with the earth's oxygen. They also carried some of the earth's atmosphere in a boxlike container on their backs.

But in the story SOMETHING WENT WRONG, and they had only a very limited amount of oxygen left on which to survive. It soon became a grave matter of life or death. The three men became fearful for their lives. One man became so afraid that he literally fought his way, against the restraint of the other two men, out of the spacecraft. They said:

"Don't go out there! You'll die.

"If you breathe the atmosphere of the moon it will kill you. You will be hurtling off in space for thousands of years—we'll never find you . . . "

Then they tried to reason with him another way by saying, "The control sta-tion on earth knows we are in trouble—and they will send a rescue craft." But he wouldn't listen and left his source of life.

Then just a short time later a rescue craft arrived, hooked onto the troubled spaceship, and started the flow of the earth's atmo-sphere into the craft of the dying men. As they began to breathe the life-giving air they were saved. But the man who refused help, who cut himself off, was lost in outer space forever.

143

And much like the astronauts, we must take the God-atmosphere with us—not in a container on our backs, but in our bodies, the temple of the Holy Spirit. This way, wherever we are, God IS. We have our being only when we have God as our dwelling place, as our personal Savior, as the divine Source of our Total Supply.

This is a powerful thought—that God IS YOUR
    DWELLING PLACE—
It's not the circumstances you are in . . .
It's not the economy of the nation or your community . . .
It's not your family or lack of family . . .
It's not the house or apartment or room you live in . . .
YOUR BEING AND YOUR DWELLING PLACE ARE
    IN GOD.

Not long ago my wife Evelyn and I were at a special gathering and a woman, whom we had known perhaps 5 years, came up and said:

"Oh, Evelyn, Oral, I'm so glad to see you. Would you come over here just a moment?"

(She had a drinking problem and she had gotten to the place where she drank alone. Her friends were concerned about her. She was a member of the church, she believed in God, but somehow she had come to a point in her life that her "being" was in alcohol. The only way she could go to a social gathering was to drink. She felt this "turned her on" for without it she was lonely even in a crowd.) She whispered, "Oral, can I have an appointment with you tomorrow?"

"What is your need?"

"You know I have a drinking problem . . . and I feel

so lonely—so isolated—I want you to really pray for my deliverance."

"Fine, what time?" She set the time. But I felt an urgency to pray immediately and I said, "Why don't we slip over here in the corner and have that prayer now?"

"In the midst of all this?—not now—tomorrow."

I turned to Evelyn and we said, "We'll see you tomorrow," and we walked away.

The next morning at the breakfast table, Evelyn said, "Oh, no! Oh, no!" and she handed me the newspaper. I read that this woman had committed suicide during the night. I don't know when I've ever been so crushed. I knew God would have saved this woman. *God could have come into her life and taken this loneliness, this isolation, away but she waited too late.* She had no being— and the reason was she had never made God her dwelling place, or her Source (Key No. 1).

When you say, "I'm all alone and nobody cares" you are telling yourself lies because the God I'm talking about has even numbered the hairs on your head (Matthew 10:30).

He knows your name.

He knows your address.

He knows your family.

He knows every pain, frustration, financial, physical or spiritual need that you have.

He loves you.

Jesus said, "I WILL NEVER LEAVE THEE NOR FORSAKE THEE" (Hebrews 13:5). There is no loneliness so bleak, no storm so fierce but that you can see Jesus there with you if you will look and START USING THE 3 KEYS. I mean by this you've got to start being something, something positive. As you do it from your heart, God will help you.

145

NOTES

10

HOW YOU
CAN LIVE
WITHOUT FEAR
IN TODAY'S WORLD

In the Prayer Tower, prayer never ceases. You may dial (918) 743-7971 any hour, day or night, 7 days a week, and receive help . . .

RECENTLY ONE OF OUR PRAYER COUNSELORS in the Prayer Tower here at ORU said:

"Brother Roberts, here's something I'd like to share with you. We received 900 phone calls today. If this continues it will be more than 5,000 calls this week. A record day was 1,045 calls. There's been a sharp rise in the number of people calling who are fearful of one thing or another."

There's fear in our country. I see and feel it in my mail. People write to me and they tell of being afraid, of not knowing what's going to happen to them next. Some of these dear people have good incomes, some are

147

broke and without a job, and some are working at hard jobs day after day just to make ends meet. Some are filled with fear even though they are very successful, and others are afraid they're not going to make it at all.

Many people fear for their families and for their children.

People are afraid of war.

Some are afraid of what's happening in our government and in our cities.

People are afraid of living and dying.

Some are afraid for their health.

Others are afraid their family will break up.

It seems that everybody is afraid of something.

But what about your life? Have you felt the hot searing pain of fear in the pit of your stomach? Do you ever become so afraid that you don't know where to turn, you don't know what to do, you don't know what to say?

Well, there's an answer for the fear in our land and for the fear and anxiety in your own life. Let me share that answer with you from my own experience and from the Bible—God's Holy Word.

GOD IS NOT THE AUTHOR OF FEAR

First, let me say that God does not want us to be afraid and to have fear dominate our lives. Fear does not come from God.

In Luke 1:71, our Lord says that He will deliver us out of the hands of our enemies that we might serve Him without fear all the days of our lives. In 2 Timothy 1:7 we see another powerful Scripture—*God hath not given us the spirit of fear; but of power, and of love, and of a sound mind.* Fear is a force of Satan that paralyzes the spirit

148

and mind of God's children—and keeps them from reaching out to God as the Source of their lives. Fear overtakes us when we look to people or things as our source and we no longer trust in God as the Source of our lives and the Source of our Total Supply (Key No. 1).

SIN IN OUR LIFE BRINGS ANXIETY AND GREAT FEAR

Let's go back to the Bible. Let's go back to the first man Adam, who became afraid and went and hid himself from God.

"Adam, why did you become afraid?"

"Because I sinned. I was ashamed and afraid, and I hid myself."

He could not face God with hidden sin in his life. His sin burdened him with great anxiety and fear.

I read about a man who had a little illegitimate child— a little girl—and nobody knew it. He kept this from most of his family for many years. But when the child was 16 years old she fell in love with his own grandson, and one of the members of the family got drunk and told all about it. It tore that family apart. Fear struck them and for weeks they lived in fear. Why? Because something back there had not been faced—something had not been brought to God, their Source. Now that's what the Bible says can happen. If you are fearful, it may be because there's something in your life that you need to open up and tell to God. Face it squarely. Repent or change your mind about it. Doing this is one of the best ways to get rid of guilt.

GIVE YOUR PAST WITH ITS MISTAKES
AND FAILURES TO GOD.

The Bible says:

As far as the east is from the west, so far hath he removed our transgressions from us (Psalm 103:12).

149

Thou wilt cast all their sins into the depths of the sea (Micah 7:19).

The first time I went around the world, I started in the west. I never reached the east because the earth is round. In these Scriptures God talks about the endless circle of His love. When you confess your sin and accept Jesus Christ as your personal Savior, your sins are forgiven. God casts them in the depths of the sea, never to be remembered against you again.

If you are not careful, you can become so upset about your past that it will destroy you. Hidden guilt will crush you; it will rob you of your faith. It will prevent you from making your own demonstration of Seed-Faith living through the 3 MIRACLE KEYS. Bring your guilt, your past sins, out into the light of God's love. Repent of your past and give it to God—He will erase it. Then, and only then, can you face the future unafraid.

"WRONG BELIEVING BRINGS FEAR INTO OUR LIVES"

I'm reminded of Charles Canty, a dear, dear partner. He's been a loyal Seed-Faith partner for nearly 15 years now. But, in his own words, he said, "My mind was tormented with fear of living and fear of dying..." Here's his story—

"A MIRACLE HAPPENED AND CHANGED EVERYTHING . . . NOW I KNOW NO DEFEAT!"

"A little over 12 years ago I lay flat on my back in the Glendale Hospital. My lungs were ravaged with tuberculosis and my mind tormented with fear—fear of dying and fear of living. I had already been in the hospital for more than a year and had seen so many in my ward die—a few minutes of strangling, more hemorrhaging and they were

150

My wife and I love to read the 3 KEYS to miracles right out of the Bible.

gone. . . . One Sunday morning I finished my breakfast and lay back to listen to the radio when a pain shot through my lungs. It felt as though they would burst. Blood gushed from my mouth and I thought, THIS IS THE END.

"It's funny the things you hear and remember when you think you're dying. The voice coming over the radio said:

> . . . *the devil has told you that*
> *you've had your last chance* . . .

I thought, *that's right, Brother!*

"After what seemed hours, but was only minutes, the hemorrhaging stopped. The voice on the radio went on . . . but I was trying to think of a way to tell my wife how to provide for our family after I was gone. I had worked in the mail department of a railroad since 1941 but had long since used up my sick leave. My family was receiving my pension—only about $45 per month—not enough to feed them, much less pay house rent. I worried day and night about them. My wife and four children were ill-clothed, ill-fed, facing possible eviction, and my debts were still piling up. **I had no place to turn to—or no one.**

"Then . . . I heard the voice on the radio say something about fear. This was when I tuned in both ears. I recognized the voice of Evangelist Oral Roberts, who had held a crusade in our city several years before. At the time, I had made light remarks about healing and miracles because I didn't need either—I was strong and healthy and didn't believe in healing or miracles. But I wasn't laughing now. I was like a drowning man reaching for a hand.

"Brother Roberts was saying:

> . . . *now it is time for the healing prayer. You there, in that hospital room, or in your home— you who are sick . . . I want you to lay your hand on your radio . . .*

I thought, I'll wait until after the prayer and then call my wife and try to find a way to tell her how to take care of herself and our children after I am gone. I never dreamed of having a miracle. I thought a miracle in my case was impossible. BUT OH! THAT PRAYER! I laid my old bony hand on that little radio and it seemed to vibrate like a drum beat. One minute I was in the valley of the shadow of death . . . . but after Brother Roberts' prayer I was in another world. It was like floating on a cloud. I can't explain it. But this I DO KNOW—THAT IN ONE DIVINE MOMENT I HAD A MIRACLE—MY LUNGS WERE HEALED!

"I wrote Brother Roberts and told him the whole story. He answered my letter and praised God with me for my miracle healing. Then he explained the 3 KEYS of Seed-Faith living. It sounded good—real good. But I came to a seminar on the ORU campus a short time later and learned more about this.

"One night during the seminar Brother Roberts was explaining the 3 KEYS to miracles. And among the many good things he said, I remembered him saying:

. . . give God your best, then ask Him for His best. Remember, the greater the sacrifice; the greater the blessing.

At first it seemed he was talking only about giving money to the Lord. But God showed me it was MORE than that. It was giving money, all right, but it was also GIVING LOVE, COMPASSION, GIVING A HELPING HAND, FAITH—in fact, OUR WHOLE LIFE.

"I had wanted a way to do something more for the Lord than I was already doing, so I decided to start 'Seed-Faith living,' as Brother Roberts called it. So I gave what I felt was 'my depth' at the time and just felt so good about it—it was my best. And soon, I began to see that the secret of a successful Christian life was in putting the 3 KEYS to work—giving God your best and putting Him FIRST in your life, seeding for a miracle by giving FIRST, and EXPECTING A MIRACLE.

"I went back home and started giving of my time—I'd go back to the hospital where I had nearly died with TB and tell the other patients what God had done for me—I'd pray with them and I led many of them to the Lord.

"Also, I was working with a group who would go to the shut-ins, the hospitals, convalescent homes—all kinds of places—giving our witness. The group kept growing and we were having a wonderful time GIVING of ourselves.

"And I just prayed a little prayer: 'Lord, it'd be wonderful if You could work out a way for me to take MORE people . . . this ol' car is about shot . . . '

"Not long after this, Brother Roberts had a partners' meeting in Delaware and we went. At this time I didn't dream of getting a new car (although I had prayed and needed one badly). But at the close of the meeting Brother Roberts walked around to each partner, laid hands on him, and prayed just a short prayer. I will never forget what happened when he got to me. He just touched my forehead lightly and said:

In Jesus' name get all your needs met NOW . . . For the next 5 minutes I felt the glow of God throughout my entire being. I didn't know what was going to happen but I knew . . .

SOMETHING GOOD WAS GOING TO HAPPEN TO ME!

Exactly 90 days after that meeting the Lord blessed me with a brand-new nine-passenger sta-

"This is where I used to live. My family was ill-clad, ill-fed, facing possible eviction, and my debts were still piling up . . . then my miracle happened."

tion wagon! And I mean, we are now IN BUSINESS FOR GOD. We take one station wagon load after another to the hospitals, to homes, to jails, to shut-ins, and it's just joy, joy, joy—all the time.

"We are now lifetime Seed-Faith partners and our lives just keep blooming.

"When I got out of the hospital in '57 our house was run-down and its value practically nothing. Well, I got busy and painted it, installed storm windows and doors, and fixed it up a little inside. We lived there a few years and then decided we would like to sell it and move to a better neighborhood. It was sold in no time at all and we received more than double what we had paid for it. With this 'overflow' we were able to pay ALL our bills, buy some new furniture, and buy a better home in a good neighborhood—right where we wanted.

"As Seed-Faith partners, we've come to know that we just don't have to accept defeat. God supplies all our needs. Sometimes these things take a little time but the Lord just seems to show me a mental picture of what He'll do for me as I really look to Him, put Him first in my life and in my giving, and EXPECT A MIRACLE EVERY DAY. It's just glorious—glorious—glorious what God is doing!"

□ □

WHEN YOU BELIEVE THAT GOD IS A GOOD GOD . . . THAT HE LOVES AND CARES FOR YOU . . . THAT HE IS A GOD OF ALL POWER . . . AND THAT HE WISHES TO USE HIS POWER ON YOUR BEHALF, THEN YOUR BELIEVING HAS CREATED FAITH IN YOUR

HEART, AND YOU CAN START USING THE
3 KEYS

This is why I love to open each of our TV programs by saying:

"SOMETHING GOOD IS GOING TO HAPPEN TO YOU." For the secret of life is in expecting miracles. We need to look for the good, to be thankful for every good thing God brings to us.

TRYING CIRCUMSTANCES CAUSE FEAR

Let's go to the New Testament and ask the disciples of our Lord Jesus about fear in their lives. Remember, they were just plain common folks like you and me today.

One evening Jesus called His disciples to Him, put them in a boat, and sent them across the Sea of Galilee ahead of Him while He went away to a mountain to pray (Matthew 14 and Mark 6).

That night while Christ was praying, the disciples were in a great storm. The winds were blowing, the waves were rolling high, the water was sucking at the little boat, and the timbers began to pop. The disciples were rubbing elbows with death and they screamed out with fear. Then, the Bible says, while Christ was on the mountain praying "HE SAW THEM TOILING [WHILE] ROWING, FOR THE WIND WAS CONTRARY" (Mark 6:48). The mind of Jesus penetrated the blackness of the terrible storm. He *saw* the little boat tossed by the waves. He *heard* the anguished cry of His own beloved disciples. That's hard to believe, isn't it? Particularly when you are so hemmed in by your problems, so desperate in your need that you wonder if God exists? If He's even within a million miles of you? Well, here in this story the storm struck suddenly and the disciples were face-to-face with death.

You know, it can happen so suddenly—the burdens, the struggles, the torments of life strike quickly . . . and then we wonder, WHERE IS GOD? But the Bible says:

"He SAW them—THEM."

Yes, Sir, from the mountain where Jesus was praying He looked down on the sea where the disciples were rubbing elbows with death, crying out in fear, and He saw them. He heard them. He felt them—THEM.

This shows us that God has made provision for us as persons—for our health, our safety, and our peace of soul. God is our Source and when we open our minds to His miracles and act on the 3 KEYS of Seed-Faith (do you know these yet?), then we will know His presence and His power—right where we need Him most.

WHEN CHRIST SAW THEM toiling in the sea and heard the rush and roar of the storm, He leaped to His feet, hurried down the mountainside, and came to the water's edge. There was no boat or bridge, so He just flung a mighty highway of faith across the trackless sea, leaped upon it; and the Bible says that He walked on the water, coming to His disciples.

THERE IS NOTHING THAT GOD WILL NOT DO IN ORDER TO COME TO YOU—IF YOU MAKE HIM YOUR SOURCE—IF YOU OPEN UP TO HIM IN YOUR FEAR AND CIRCUM-STANCES—AND IF YOU EXPECT—YES, EXPECT, HELP FROM GOD

So many don't expect, you know. You can. I can.

Christ came walking upon the water. But the disciples didn't recognize Him. They saw a silhouette balanced upon the stormy waves.

"It's a spirit!" they cried.

"It's a ghost!" they shrieked in fear. Then there came across the waves the compelling voice of Jesus:

"It is I; be not afraid."

In other words, *I am the Source for the saving of your life. You need not fear because I've come to you at the point of your great need . . . with the miracle you need in the NOW of your life.*

It reminds me of a little boy who was given a part to play in the church play. It was this Scripture that Jesus gave us, "It is I; be not afraid."

His mother coached him and he learned his lines. He went to the church that night and it came his time to speak. He walked out on the stage, but suddenly everything was different. There were the bright lights and the big crowd, and he didn't feel his mother near and he panicked. He hadn't anticipated seeing all those bright lights and all the people, so he just stood there. It was a terribly embarrassing silence.

Pretty soon, from behind the curtain, there was a prompting voice that said, "It is I; be not afraid."

Still the little boy just stood there. And again the prompter said, "It is I; be not afraid." Finally he gulped and blurted out, "It's only me, and I'm scared to death."

I tell you, that's the way we get. "Look, it's only me, and I'm scared out of my wits." Any man that doesn't admit he gets scared is not telling the truth. Because we all face storms in our lives—but let me tell you, there's Somebody else concerned about us.

Today we need to listen. To get quiet. So we can hear Jesus saying to us, "Be not afraid; it is I." Many people are hearing it. THE VOICE OF JESUS CAN ACTUALLY BE HEARD THE STRONGEST WHEN OUR BACKS

ARE AGAINST THE WALL . . . WHEN WE HAVE NO PERSON OR NO THING WE CAN TURN TO. That is when God our Source says, through His Son Jesus of Nazareth, "Be of good cheer; it is I; be not afraid." You can hear it if you expect to, and if you listen.

Why didn't the disciples recognize Him? Why was He shrouded in a cloak of misunderstanding? Why weren't they able to see Him as He really is? They failed to recognize Him because they were not expecting Him to appear. That could be your trouble today. Perhaps you are not getting your miracles because your mind is still on the problem, on the fear, and you are not OPENING YOUR MIND to miracles.

You must put in seed faithfully . . . look to God as your only real and faithful Source . . . and expect the miracles that you need!

You must *expect* your miracle of supply and deliverance. In this way, you can avoid fear entering your heart and shutting you off from your Source, our blessed Lord. God performed miracles through Jesus on the front streets and the dusty roads, in the fields and houses and vineyards and shops, and then on the waters of the Holy Land . . . He did it because many people finally looked beyond their sickness and fear and loneliness and financial need because they started EXPECTING Him to meet their needs. Because they finally fixed their eyes upon the real Source for their lives. It still works like that TODAY because Jesus operates best in a feeling of expectancy you have about Him (Key No. 3).

O O O

Al Jessen lived with fear most of his life. He had a severe breakdown several years ago and had never fully recovered. He thought of suicide many times. Somehow he managed to carry on with his work but he awoke each morning dreading the torment of that day. He attended church regularly but there was a great emptiness in his life because he had never accepted Christ as Savior. (So many dear people who go to church never seem to have the Church live in them.)

Then, one day, someone sent him a subscription to the ABUNDANT LIFE magazine. With that magazine came a ray of hope. Each month when it came, he would stop everything and read it from cover to cover.

One Sunday morning he was in the yard working when an inner voice said to him:

"Go into the house and turn on the radio to the Fargo, North Dakota, station."

Now it was usually impossible for him to get this station in this particular area, but Al went in and turned on

Al Jessen and Lee Braxton at a seminar

160

the radio anyway. He could just barely hear a voice so he got down in front of the radio and said:

"God, if You want me to hear this, You will have to make it come in clear enough so I can." Immediately it came in loud and clear.

That broadcast was a turning point in Al's life. Later he told me:

"Brother Roberts, that day you preached a message which dealt with my exact trouble—fear, depression, and anxiety. It seemed you were talking just to me! And your healing prayer at the end of the program went right to the point of my need.

IN THE MIDST OF MY DEPRESSION, SICKNESS, AND FEAR, GOD PUT HIS GREAT BIG HAND ON MY LIFE

I got up and went outside, knowing that the Lord had given me a miracle. I felt such relief in my mind! I looked up to the open sky and thanked God for speaking to me. The spirit of depression lifted and a definite healing began. But I still didn't really know the One who had healed me— the Great Physician.

"Then I was invited to a laymen's seminar on the campus of Oral Roberts University. From the time I arrived on the campus I felt an atmosphere charged with the love and Spirit of God. Nothing in my life has ever had the influence on me that the seminar had.

"For it was there that I met MY GREAT PHYSICIAN! I accepted Jesus as Lord of my life. The burden of sin I had carried so many years lifted. Such joy flooded my soul! At last

161

I knew the Lord not only as my Healer, but also as my Savior. I felt a completeness!

"Today I'm living for God. I claim victory over the enemies of my life in the name of Jesus. I LOOK TO HIM AS MY SOURCE. I AM LIVING SEED-FAITH EVERY DAY."

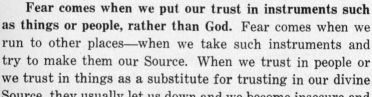

Fear comes when we put our trust in instruments such as things or people, rather than God. Fear comes when we run to other places—when we take such instruments and try to make them our Source. When we trust in people or we trust in things as a substitute for trusting in our divine Source, they usually let us down and we become insecure and afraid—fear dominates us. I want you to notice Peter's reaction when Christ arrived, walking on the water. Peter is standing in the boat, with it being tossed, and decides he doesn't want to be in the boat any longer. He realizes how unreliable, how unsafe and dangerous it is. He says:

"If it is really You, Lord Jesus, bid me come to You on the water."

He saw that Christ was the Source of his Total Supply to be delivered from that storm. The Man out there on the water was more safe and reliable than the boat in which he was being tossed. This is the great difference between instrument and Source. People get their eyes upon certain instruments, and when those instruments fail them they often lose their faith. An instrument is just that—no more, no less; whereas, God is Source. He cannot fail. If you look to God as Source and one instrument fails, God will use another. *But God shall supply all your need* (Philippians

4:19) (Key No. 1). The only true Strength—the only reliable Source—is God.

LEARN TO TRUST YOUR SOURCE

A crack airline pilot almost failed his first solo flight because he didn't trust his plane. He got it off the ground, up in the air, but then the instructor saw the plane begin to wobble and dip. He ran frantically back and forth on the field, signaling the pilot to land. Finally, he somehow made a landing.

"What in the world were you doing up there?" the instructor asked.

"I tell you, Sir. I just couldn't rest my full weight on the seat. When I got up there and saw how big the sky was and how little my plane was, I just couldn't see how it could fly. To tell the truth, I was getting up and down, bumping my head against the ceiling—I just couldn't trust it."

The instructor said, "That airplane is MADE to fly. You don't have to fly it—just adjust the instruments, put your full weight down on the seat and it will fly itself!!!"

How many times have we done the same thing with God? We say, God is our Source, but by our actions we say that we aren't quite sure we can trust Him.

God is saying to us, "I am your Source. You've got to TRUST ME. Lean back on Me. Put your full weight on Me."

Rest your full weight on God "casting all your care upon him; for he careth for you" (1 Peter 5:7). I know it's not easy. I'm not going to say that it is but I know it can be done. Every one of us has done it at some time, haven't we? But we need to learn to do it more often and for longer periods of time. As we do, our fear will decrease and our faith will increase. Now say it with me:

GOD IS THE SOURCE OF MY TOTAL SUPPLY.
I REST MY FULL WEIGHT ON HIM.
(Memorize this and say it often.)

It's so important to you to learn to trust God as your Source in all areas of your life, to continually apply Key No. 1.

For Lee Braxton, a Christian layman and one of my dear longtime associates in this ministry, applying the 3 KEYS to his total life meant the difference between life and death. Lee flies his own plane—traveling thousands of miles each year ministering to our partners. When he returned from one such trip he shared this experience with me:

"I started to land when the nose landing gear on the

Lee Braxton

164

plane failed to lock in place. We immediately recognized the possibility of severe injury or death.

"I knew it would take more than my skill to get us out of this situation. We circled the field for 2 hours while preparations were being made for our landing.

"**Suddenly I thought about God as my source of protection.** We joined hands in a brief prayer. In our prayer I reminded God that He was our source of protection, and we were His servants trying to do His will. For years we had been sowing seed and now I believed God my Source to give me divine wisdom and skill to make a safe landing.

"Fire trucks, ambulances, nurses, a National Guard rescue squad, and many others were there waiting to help us—when we got down. The runway had been foamed to reduce the fire hazard of the metal skidding on the concrete. The airport was closed to all other traffic—and I was cleared to land. Coming in at a jetlike speed, I attempted a landing. We touched down on the foamed part of the runway. The nose dropped gently and the plane skidded to a halt a short distance away.

"The plane sustained a minimum of damage <u>but not a one of us suffered even a scratch</u>!

"We were deeply grateful to everyone who stood by to aid us in case of disaster, but we all knew a hand greater than mine guided that disabled plane to a safe landing."

O O O

If you are fearful today, ask yourself these questions:

1. <u>Is there something in my life that I need to confess to God</u>? Have I repented of my hidden sins and asked God's forgiveness—

so they will burden and fill me with guilt no more?

2. Are negative thoughts destroying my faith, or am I building faith in my heart by right believing? Believing that God is a good God . . . that He loves and cares for me . . . that He is a God of all power . . . and that He wishes to use His power on my behalf?

3. Have I allowed circumstances to hide the face of God, the Source of my Total Supply? Have I recognized this moment that God is in the NOW of my need, that He sees me, He feels what I am going through, and He comes to walk me through the circumstances?

4. Am I really trusting in God, the Source of my Total Supply? (Key No. 1). Am I resting my full weight on Him?

5. Am I filling my mind and my life with Jesus Christ—the One who is qualified to take all my fears because He sat where I sit . . . and He gave first? Am I focusing my attention on Him who is the healing for all my fears and the miracle-giver for all my needs?

11 HOW THE SECOND TOUCH OF JESUS CAN HEAL YOUR INNER MAN

(and how it affected the relationship between my son Richard and me)

THE OTHER DAY I picked up the paper and read where a famous man in America said, "So-and-so is a son-of-a —." That's pretty tough language even in private, but to read it in a newspaper!!! Did you ever think how dehumanizing and demoralizing it is to consider a human being, made in God's image, in this way?

As men, we tend to depersonalize people. We look upon others as just cogs in a machine, numbers, a part of that great mass of humanity called mankind. God made everybody to be somebody. He didn't make anyone to be a nobody.

Everybody is a special person made in the image of God. Each of us, as an individual, is of infinite worth—so much so that Christ died for us as persons. And yet we are not so important that we are better or greater than our brother or our sister. We belong to God and belonging to God we belong to one another, and belonging to one another we belong to ourselves. Therefore, it is important that we develop a right relationship with God and with each other. This is only possible through the healing power of Jesus Christ.

LET JESUS GIVE YOU A SECOND TOUCH

Jesus Christ healed many people, including blind people. We are told in Mark 8:23-25 about a blind man whom Jesus had to touch twice. He touched the blind man and said, "Can you see?"

"Yes. I see men as trees walking."

Jesus touched the man a second time, then asked him what he saw.

"I see men clearly," answered the blind man.

This suggests that there are two kinds of healing that we need in life.

One is the physical. And one is for the inner man. The first touch of Jesus was for the blind man's eyes. But even though his eyes were opened, inwardly he still had the same biases and prejudices that he'd had before his eyes were healed.

That second touch was necessary because he saw people as TREES, as something to cut down, to run over—to reduce to ashes—he treated them as things! He needed a second touch so he could be sensitive to people, to have a right relationship with them. He needed to get into a people-world and learn how to live in it.

Even if you have 20-20 vision, perfect eyesight, you don't always SEE what you ought to see. You may think your problem is physical and attempt to correct it through surgery. The operation may be successful. Your body may respond but you may still have the same old prejudice, bitterness, and hate inside that you had before. You may feel better in your body and yet not feel better toward people, those you live with, those you see every day. You are not living with trees, you are living with PEOPLE. YOU NEED THE SECOND TOUCH SO YOU CAN SEE PEOPLE AS HUMAN BEINGS, SO THAT YOUR RELATIONSHIPS CAN BE HEALED.

Nowhere is there a greater need for the healing of relationships today than in our homes. You can count on your fingers the number of families in our country who don't have problems with their children. Or children who don't have problems with their parents. It seems like it is that kind of age, and a minister's family is no exception.

A Scripture that I have tried to live by, and that has the 3 KEYS in it, is Matthew 6:33, "But seek ye first the kingdom of God . . . and all these things shall be added unto you." I have tried to put God first in my life, to come under God's authority, to do what He has called me to do by putting in the seed, then trusting that He would take care of my family, that my children would become Christians and serve God, and that they would make something of their lives. In this way, I have expected miracles to happen to each of them.

Having been called into this ministry, I have had to travel throughout the world and be gone from home much of the time. Really, my wife Evelyn raised our four children. When I was home I was with the children a lot. I played with them and I taught them the Scriptures. But I was gone so much. Sometimes Evelyn would go with me because I would get so lonesome, especially when I was overseas for several weeks at a time.

We had babysitters to stay with our children; sometimes it worked out and sometimes it didn't. I remember when we went to Australia, I said, "Honey, go with me if you can. I will be over there a long time . . . maybe we can get someone to stay with the children."

Richard was just a little boy at that time. When we came home from Australia I went into his bedroom and discovered that someone had chopped off the bedpost. I said, "What happened?"

The lady who had stayed with the children said, "Well, Richard was upset because you and his mother were gone so he took his little hatchet and cut off the bedpost."

I wanted to "wear him out" but I couldn't, to save my life.

As Richard grew up a gap grew between us. He began to sing for coffeehouses and to lean toward show business. The more I wanted him to sing for me in the ministry, the less he wanted to. One Sunday morning I asked him to sing for one of our seminars at ORU and he said, "No, Dad, I don't want to sing for you."

It shouldn't have hurt me, but it did. It really got down inside. When children are little they step on your toes, but when they are older they step on your heart.

Then Richard went off to a state university. I could understand his not particularly wanting to attend ORU when his father was president. He was away from home for the first time on his own, and doing his own thing. I was back home, still traveling, still thinking about him, and praying and wondering about his gifted voice which was being developed more fully all the time.

Then one day he came home. He said, "Dad, let's go out and play a game of golf." We went out on the golf course and he was hitting the ball "a mile." He is a tremendous golfer. (I'm a pretty good golfer myself once in a while but I couldn't hit the ball that day because I was all bound up inside. My mind was not on the game.) As I talked to Richard I could see he was turning me off. Finally, I said, "OK, Richard, let's just go home." So we picked up our clubs right in the midst of the game and headed for the car. We sat there and just glared at each other. And I will remember his words as long as I live.

He said, "Dad, get off my back!—AND GET OUT OF MY LIFE!!"

Then it came to me that maybe I *was* on his back; maybe *I* was trying to save him. I was not trusting in my Source to do it. I thought about it a moment. I calmed down and I began to silently pray "in the spirit." Confidentially, I didn't know what to say to God with my own understanding (1 Corinthians 14:15).

Then I said, "OK, Richard, give me your hand." With his hand in mine, I said, "From this moment I am off your back. I am going to put you in the hands of God."

I felt then it was God's battle and not mine. The One who is my Total Supply had him. A relief came over me. Richard went back to the university. Outwardly nothing had changed, but I had put the 3 KEYS to work and I was expecting a miracle.

Then one day his mother received a phone call and Richard said, "Mother, do you suppose that Oral Roberts University would accept me for next year?"

She asked me and I said, "I don't know, Evelyn." Richard had taken up a habit or two and later, when he came to me, I told him he couldn't do the things he was doing and be a student on the ORU campus.

He said, "I can quit."

I said, "That will be up to you."

There is a point in dealing with your children when it has to be at arm's length. You are no longer emotionally involved. They are released to God and you can act without fear. The Holy Spirit operating in your life takes the gift of faith and drops it into your heart so that you can look upon your problems from the vantage point of God himself and believe as God believes. You can expect miracles (Key No. 3).

171

Richard enrolled at ORU, and he followed the rules of the campus. But we were still having problems. Then he fell in love with Patti, the girl who is now his wife.

Shortly before their wedding date something happened to their line of communication, particularly in spiritual matters. Although Patti was very much in love with Richard, she knew they didn't have a chance if they got bogged down there. She told him, "Richard, there's a special kind of communication between Christians—and a very special kind between a Christian man and woman who plan to be married. They are of one mind and their utmost goal is to serve the Lord and to live the way He wants them to live. I feel that somehow we are missing each other on this. If our communication breaks down here, it will break down in other areas of our lives. This frightens me. I know you are a Christian and if you die you will go to heaven, but of what earthly

Patti Roberts

good are you to God? I know our plans are all finalized but unless something changes, I'll have to call off the wedding."

She later told me, "I was searching for an inner commitment in Richard that said, 'Lord if You call me to the wilds of Africa, or to Brazil, or wherever, I will go because I love You.'"

At the time, Evelyn happened to be with me in California. She said, "Oral, I feel impressed to go home." When she has these feelings I never oppose her. She got on a plane and was home within a few hours.

Richard was living in the dorm on campus at the time. His mother hadn't been home but a short time when he walked into the house. He said, "Mother, I'm so glad you are home. I've got to talk to you."

Evelyn said, "What is the trouble, Richard?"

"**Well, something has happened to Patti.** She can't seem to understand that I love her, and I really do."

Then he said, "Mother, she is going to call the wedding off."

Evelyn said, "Well, Richard, when you committed your life to the Lord recently, did you say, 'Lord, I will live for You if You will give me Patti?' You can't compromise with God. God wants all of you, or nothing. Now He may, or may not give you Patti. You can live without Patti but you can't live without the Lord. The Lord wants all of you without reservations."

Then he got down on his knees and put his head in his mother's lap like he used to when he was a little boy, and they really prayed. And something happened inside Richard. He looked up, smiling through his tears, and he said, "It is all right, Mother. It is all right. I don't want to give up Patti, but if that is the way the Lord wants it I must serve God regardless."

Then he picked up the phone and called me in California. He said, "Dad, everything is OK now."

I knew what he meant. "Dad, you are not on my back anymore."

The next morning Richard saw Patti and he started to tell her what had happened. But he didn't have to tell her. She said, "I was praying last night, too. And suddenly that heaviness lifted. I knew something had happened. I didn't know what, exactly, but I wasn't worried anymore. Richard, I am ready to marry you."

They were married in November 1968. It has been a joy to Evelyn and me to see them putting God first in their total lives—their home, their time, their giving, and especially their talents. Richard is now ordained and deeply involved in God's work with me. Although they now have two beautiful baby girls, they still take time to minister and they are touching the hearts of thousands with their consecrated singing talents as they minister with us on our television programs and hour-long TV specials, as well as on tour with the ORU World Action Singers.

On one of our TV programs I asked, "Richard, do you still think I'm on your back?"

He smiled and said, "No, Dad. You're no longer on my back but I'm by your side."

174

Well, this Scripture is really true, "Seek ye first the kingdom of God . . . and all these things shall be added unto you." We have been tested and we will be tested again, but I'm so grateful for this Scripture that if we seek God and put Him first, if we make God the Source, and if we are constantly opening up and putting in the seed of our INNER SELF and expecting a miracle . . . expecting God to take a hand in the situation . . . wonderful things will happen in our inner man and our relationship with our family and with people.

WHEN JESUS GAVE HIMSELF ON THE CROSS HE OPENED UP A NEW DIMENSION OF LOVE— "PEOPLE" LOVE!

Listen, Jesus is in the now. He paid the ultimate price to heal a broken relationship. He went to the cross, and there on the cross He gave himself for you, for me, and for every man. And when Jesus Christ gave himself on the cross He opened up a new dimension of love, "PEOPLE" LOVE—an acceptance of ourselves and of others—first, just as we are, and then as He can make us to become.

In the Old Testament it was "an eye for an eye and a tooth for a tooth." If someone struck you, you struck back. But in the New Testament Jesus said, "Love your neighbor as yourself. Do good to them that despitefully use you."

Loving others begins with loving yourself. For the way you act toward others is a reflection of your inward feelings toward yourself. God gives you the ability to accept yourself as a worthy person. You can be at peace with yourself. You see, God does not despise you because you are human. God loves humanity because He made it. God wants to reach down through the HOLY SPIRIT into every cell of your being and bring you to your highest potential. When you are able to see yourself as a person that God loves, even though you have faults and limitations, then you will be able to accept and love others in spite of their faults and limitations.

"PEOPLE" LOVE WILL CHANGE YOU!

We had a student at ORU who was an UNHOLY terror. He gave his professors trouble; he gave the students trouble. He just didn't get along with anybody. He was a pain in the neck of everyone. All the things that were done to discipline him rolled off him like water off a duck's back. After everybody else had tried to help him they sent him to me. I listened to his side of the story. I talked with him—all the time I was searching for a way to get through to him. Then I felt impressed to say, "I'm going to fine you $20." (That may not seem like much to you, but it is a lot to a student who is broke.)

Let me tell you. That got his attention. He began to wilt. I hit him right at the nerve end of his billfold. I knew immediately that I had found the key.

He stood up and paced the room. Finally, he said, "What am I going to do? I don't have $20. I'll have to leave school."

There was a long, long silence—you could almost read his mind—"What'll I tell my parents when they see me coming through the front door? . . . " And probably a dozen other thoughts. After what seemed like an hour, one of the members of the administration spoke up and said, "I'll pay the fine for you." That really broke him up.

"You mean you'll pay my fine after the way I've been acting?" I wish you could have seen the change in that boy! He became one of the best students we ever had. We had a miracle walking around on the ORU campus—I mean a human being! He began to love the students and love the faculty—he even liked the president! The campus pastor told me later that this student said, "FOR THE FIRST TIME IN MY LIFE, I LOVE PEOPLE." I've never seen a more practical and successful demonstration of the 3 KEYS by all concerned than in that tough situation.

When you see men, what do you see? Do you see them as white, black, yellow, brown, red? What do you see? What do you call them? You know, it's pretty hard to shake hands with a tree. And it's pretty hard to build a marriage when people look like trees to you. It's pretty hard to build any kind of relationship when people look like trees to you because trees are something people often cut down or burn down. And when we cut on one another, or reduce someone to a thing or an object, we are "seeing men as trees."

NOW WHAT CAN WE DO ABOUT THIS? HOW CAN WE SEE CLEARLY? HOW CAN WE BE HEALED IN THE INNER MAN? Let me give you three or four Bible suggestions:

Number one, let's get completely honest and admit we sometimes see people as trees. Get completely frank. Admit your need. I have to do this all the time—admit my need. I believe God can change things in your life. What is it you are facing? What's hurting you the most? Is it something someone is doing to you; is it something you are doing to someone else, or is it both? Does the color of someone's skin make you see him as a tree? Or because he's somehow different from you?

Number two, let's realize that we will always be partly blind until we ask Jesus for a second touch. Only

177

He loves everybody with the same love and treats them all with respect and concern.

Number three, let's realize that only Christ our Source can heal our inner man through the power of the Holy Spirit.

Number four, let's realize we have to definitely use Key No. 2 here and put seeds of love in toward all people, and I mean all.

12 HOW TO RECEIVE A MIRACLE TO MAKE YOUR MARRIAGE LIVE AGAIN

LEARNING TO GIVE FIRST stopped a cold war in the Kilstrand home. "Our marriage wasn't exactly on the rocks," Dennis told me; "it was more like a 'cold war.' The warmth and affection had gone out of our relationship. Kathy and I walked *around* each other rather than touching, or smiling, or speaking. I wanted her to give me her attention and affection. And she felt *I* should do some giving first. As a result, neither of us would take the first step.

"Then one morning your telecast came on. You were telling about a young couple who had fallen out of love. Every point you made was as though you were reading from our own personal list of troubles.

"At the close of the program you asked everyone to join hands with the person they were with, and pray with you. We squirmed uncomfortably. Kathy sort of glanced at me and I glanced back. Actually, we felt embarrassed. But we decided right then and there to put our personal feelings aside.

"Kathy said, 'OK, let's pray with him.'

"And I said, 'Why not?'

"And we did. And from that moment, our whole rela-

The Kilstrands—Kathy and Dennis

tionship began to change. It was only in small ways at first. When I'd come home in the evenings Kathy would have the house shining, and be in the kitchen humming softly as she prepared the evening meal. She'd greet me with a smile and a kiss. And I found myself giving in return, being more thoughtful, helping with the children and the house. AND ONE DAY WE REALIZED THAT WE WERE IN LOVE AGAIN! The whole atmosphere of our home changed, but not until we started giving FIRST, that day we prayed with you, as you asked your viewers to do.

"Then we wrote for your book, MIRACLE OF SEED-FAITH, and read it. That book gave us a clearer understanding of the 3 KEYS of Seed-Faith living. And through the months we have found that it works—not only in our marriage, but in every area of our lives."

MANY PEOPLE SAY, "MARRIAGE IS A 50-50 PROPOSITION."

In other words, a partnership—you come half way and I'll come half way. I'll do my part and you do your part. I believe the New Testament teaches that marriage is a 100 percent proposition. Jesus said, "GIVE, FIRST." And there is no limitation set—it is a totality of giving. Give and keep on giving until you receive the miracle you need.

This reminds me of the woman who wrote me and asked, "Just how far do I have to go with this 'giving first?'" It seems that she had already filed for divorce—her marriage had been stormy for some time. Her husband would beat her so severely that at times the neighbors would call the police. Finally, in despair of his ever changing, she left him and filed for a divorce.

Spiritually, mentally, and physically . . . she had come to the end of her rope. In her desperation she wrote me for prayer, and I wrote her back saying that I was praying for her and encouraging her to believe God for a miracle. In one letter I reminded her of the fishermen (in Luke 5) who had toiled all night and taken nothing, and then the Lord came along and said, "Let down your net . . . just one more time."

In her letter back to me she said:

Dear Brother Roberts:

When your letter came I was in the same frame of mind as those fishermen must have been. I wanted to believe but I hardly dared to. Then there were

181

your words, "Let down your net--one more time."
I'm crying as I write this letter. I want you to
pray with me that my husband will accept Christ
and that we can be reunited.

WITHIN DAYS, THE MIRACLE BEGAN.
I received another letter:

Dear Brother Roberts:

Just a few days after I sent you that letter,
the miracle began. My husband came by and wanted
to talk with me. We talked but got nowhere, so I
said:

"Take me home. Let's hang it up."

Instead he drove to our pastor's home, which
was a miracle because in times past he had told the
pastor to stay out of our business. The pastor and
his wife talked to us for 2 hours (while friends
prayed). Then my husband asked:

"What can I do to save our marriage?"

Our pastor told him that he should begin by
committing his life to Christ. Later we all knelt
and prayed and he accepted Christ as his Savior.
And he became a changed man. God did give us a
whole net full of miracles...We cancelled our
divorce. Today our home is full of love. How I
thank you for your ministry and prayers.

Jesus Christ didn't ask anything from anybody until
He had given to them first
    ... until He gave himself,
        ... His life,
            ... His time,
                ... His talent,

182

       ... His eternal love,

           ... everything He had.

God himself called His Son "the seed of David." Jesus was a seed-sower first. And by His example we can learn that—

> **The way to a person's heart**
> **is to give first—**
> **to put a seed in.**

Sometimes we THINK we <u>are</u> giving. But when we really let God examine our hearts He shows us that maybe there is more we can do—like the woman who wrote me concerning her husband who was an alcoholic. She told how they were considering divorce. In my answer to her <u>I asked if she had ever considered seeding for a miracle in her marriage</u> by going out of her way to give her husband some love and consideration FIRST. Well, she began by opening her heart to God and praying that God would change <u>her husband</u> so they could have a happy home again.

So she prayed...

    and prayed...

        and prayed.

In her letter to me she said:

> Then one day God opened my mind and let me see all the mistakes I had made--the many times I had failed to <u>give</u> my husband the assurance of my love that he so desperately needed. My inner vision was buried under tons of self-pity. I was saying, in effect, "If you don't love me, I won't love you." I was expecting to receive his love and attention without first giving to him.
>
> I was a good Christian (or so I thought). I took the children to church regularly but I

183

*just "walked out around" my husband. My life
was completely separated from him. Actually I
suppose I was wrapped in a cloak of self-righteousness.
But I soon realized how he could find no place for
himself in my life and, even worse, our children
were following my example.*

*Thank God! Through your letters and the 3 KEYS
of Seed-Faith living I finally saw the light! I
asked God's forgiveness. And I thank Him daily
for helping me to see my mistakes.*

*IT HASN'T BEEN AN INSTANT TRANSFORMATION IN
OUR MARRIAGE. It isn't easy to express feelings
that we've smothered for so long but we are both
working at it. We have had some long talks, trying
to regain the love we had during our first years
of marriage. I'M NOT ASKING FOR HIS LOVE, JUST
ASSURING HIM OF MINE BY GIVING LOVINGLY TO HIM.
When I do something for him or smile and say
something nice, it's like seeing a small part of
glory when his eyes light up!*

*He hasn't taken a drink in a long time now.
I know it's a struggle for him. But he's fighting!
Now he has started going to church! That is another
of God's miracles! I'm so happy I just can't be still.
Learning to seed for a miracle by giving first made
all the difference.*

Yes, miracles will happen in your home when you begin
to practice the 3 KEYS of Seed-Faith living—where it
really counts—when you begin to give of yourself . . .
when you truly make God your Source and the center of
your home.

Now when you give something it's important that you don't expect to receive back from the person you give to. Your spouse is not your Source; he or she is only an instrument. Whatever you give must become an act toward God!

For it is God who heals marriages,
> it is God who changes people—
>> both you and your spouse—
> it is God who can renew the love in your hearts again.

But it all begins with your giving, and giving FIRST. And you can't do this without God's love. Surrender your life to Christ. Take Him into your life and into your heart as your personal Savior. Follow Jesus, give as He gave, love as He loved, let Him help you to forgive as He forgives. Then start expecting miracle after miracle after miracle (Key No. 3).

□ □

TURN ON TO FORGIVING FIRST

It was not until Sue turned on to the possibility of a miracle of forgiveness that a healing of her relationship with Harold began, and their marriage was saved. Many considered their marriage to be an ideal one—they had three lovely children and Harold was a good provider. But on the inside, their marriage was falling apart because Sue could not forgive him for having been unfaithful. They both attended church regularly and were Christians but had never opened their mind to the possibility of a miracle in their marriage. As a result, they separated—both feeling that a reconciliation was impossible.

In the meantime, Sue got hold of MIRACLE OF SEED-

185

FAITH. And in the midst of her hurt and brokenness, Sue began to read the book. One day she said:

"God, I don't know how You can heal our marriage. With me, it's impossible. With Harold, it's impossible. But with You, all things are possible."

As she shared with me how God gave her a miracle, she said:

"I think, under normal circumstances I just would have come unglued because I'm a very emotional person. But I had given myself BACK TO GOD FIRST. Then I gave some of my earnings as Seed-Faith—an amount that meant something to me. I then looked to God as the Source of my Total Supply. Then I really began to expect a miracle for our broken marriage. I mean I put the 3 KEYS to a real test with my faith.

"The first tangible result was that GOD BROUGHT A CALMNESS TO MY SPIRIT. I was able to go to work every day with peace of mind, and also care for my family.

"However, as each day passed, the miracle I had 'seeded' for, and needed most, seemed further out of reach than ever. Other problems began to pile up. My sister died. Strife arose in our church. Then other problems came up in the family. It was just one hurt on top of another. But I clung to the Scripture, 'But my God shall supply all— ALL—YOUR NEED . . . ' (Philippians 4:19)."

"Go to a marriage counselor? Never!"

"Then one day the Lord strongly impressed me to go talk to our family physician about our situation. He directed me to a Christian counseling center. 'Get Harold to go to a marriage counselor?—Never!' I didn't think Harold would even consider it. In fact, I nearly decided not to mention it. But there was my miracle again. I asked, and he agreed to go. IT WASN'T EASY FOR EITHER OF

186

US but we felt this was God directing us. The Lord used this Christian counselor to help us SEE ourselves. We both began to see also that God had HIS way to put us back together. And eventually that which was broken was healed . . . in both of us. WITH OUR MARRIAGE AND HOME RESTORED AND FIRMLY CENTERED IN GOD, WE FOUND ALMOST DAILY THAT WE WERE DRAWN CLOSER TO GOD. This was a new experience for us. Now that God has become our Source, it seems natural to look to God our SOURCE daily and to expect miracles for all our needs."

What Sue found was that the long weeks and months of casting her bread upon the waters did come to her MULTIPLIED again . . . and again . . .

The very power that
successful marriages are built on
—and thrive on—is L-O-V-E-!!!

WHAT TO DO WHEN YOU PRAY FOR MIRACLES IN YOUR MARRIAGE AND STILL FEEL FORSAKEN OF GOD . . .

John and Ruth Gervase didn't have much going for them.

John had terminal cancer and 2 to 6 months to live . . .
Ruth was recovering from a nervous breakdown . . .
They went to church—read the Bible—prayed—
    NOTHING!
Both felt forsaken of God.
Steeped in their own need and self-pity . . .

187

Ruth and John Gervase

Seemingly, their marriage was hopelessly shattered. In spite of three lovely children, they both wanted out... Then one day Ruth suggested to John that they go to an Oral Roberts Crusade hundreds of miles away from their home.

John's response was, "You know how I feel about that stuff."

Not long after this, John came home and Ruth was gone . . . Her note read:

Dear John, I know you don't agree with what I'm doing, but I have to do it because I feel that it's right. I'm going to the crusade for prayer that you will be healed...

John tossed the note aside and said to himself, "What'll she think of next?"

Later Ruth shared how God met her at the crusade: "The Lord had let me see how selfish I had been in thinking only of myself when John was really so ill. Suddenly at the crusade my heart welled up with an overwhelming love for John and a God-given faith for his healing. It didn't seem strange at all that I was there, hundreds of miles from home. I knew now in my heart, the instant you prayed John's healing would begin.

"You preached on 'The Fourth Man' that night—about the three Hebrew children who were facing the fiery furnace. And during your message you pointed to the audience and said, 'Those of you out there who are facing a fiery furnace, are you able to say that God is able to deliver you?' I sat there drinking it all in and said simply, 'Yes, God'—just like that.

I had written on my prayer card for a complete healing of cancer for my husband, and a healing of our marriage.

"Just about the time this was taking place, John was watching TV at home and the thought crossed his mind, *it would be nice if that healing thing really worked.* Then he thought, *it must be over by now.* And then he experienced something new—his legs were always tingly; they felt like they were asleep—real bad asleep. Every night he looked forward to falling asleep just so he wouldn't feel this terrible tingling. But now he thought, *I'll try to stand on my toes.* Before this he had tried about ten times a day, without success. But this particular night he tried it again, and stood on his right toes for the first time in at least a year."

The next day Ruth called John and asked him to meet her at the bus depot. John said later, "It was terribly foggy. I could barely see to drive but I made it, and walked down all those steps without limping or falling. My legs were not completely healed, but I was able to do things I had not been able to do for a year. I believe my legs began to heal from the moment my wife and Brother Roberts prayed together for me the night before. Walking without falling or limping was proof enough that I was on my way. I could feel it inside me.

"The last checkup I had was in July and the doctor said,

'You're one of our winners, John—you're going to make it.'

"And I told the doctor the whole story. I thanked him for the help he had given me, then I thanked the greatest Physician of all.

"Our marriage was on its way back again, too.

Ruth's first act of giving of faith and love toward me was the beginning.

"Shortly after this she went to a prayer retreat and received the baptism in the Holy Spirit. She really became a new person. When I saw the change that the Holy Spirit made in her, things took on a whole new meaning in our relationship.

"I can't stop telling people about what has happened to us. We are happier than we have ever been. Not only did God heal my body and Ruth's emotions, but He healed our marriage and our home that we thought was broken beyond repair because of that first seed of giving that Ruth planted for me."

THE HOLY SPIRIT CAN MAKE YOUR HOUSE A HOME

Recently Leo and Doris Fenton shared with me how receiving a deeper relationship with Jesus Christ helped them to truly "see" each other and brought a healing of their marriage. They had been married for nearly 20 years but, in their own words, the only thing they had in common was their children. He went his way; she went hers. There was a great gulf between them. In the past they had been regular church attendants, but they had become bitter and in disappointment turned away from the church altogether. Even 10-year-old Brian denied believing in God.

The Fenton family

In the midst of this vacuum of misery, Doris turned on the television one day and heard our telecast. She began to write to me and ask questions from the Bible, and I would write her back and answer these questions. Even as I wrote, I sensed that God was trying to break through in this family's life—that the questions she asked were not the real problems at all. We were planning a seminar at ORU about that time, so I sent them an invitation.

In the meantime a friend invited Leo to attend church with him, and to Leo's own surprise—that night he accepted Christ. Leo later told me, "When I went home that night and told Doris, she just laughed. She didn't know any more about salvation than I did. But I knew something had happened in my life. <u>I had met Someone—Jesus Christ!</u> I guess that is why I wanted to attend the seminar at ORU!"

Well, Leo came to the seminar, along with about 500

others from all over America, and while he was waiting to register in the lobby another guest came up to him and started talking to him about the Holy Spirit. This was entirely new to him, so he asked many questions. That night I spoke on Seed-Faith and at the close of the service I asked if anyone was interested in discussing the baptism in the Holy Spirit.

In telling about receiving this experience, Leo said, "I put up my hand, with about a third of the crowd, because I was curiously interested. In the counseling room Dr. Howard Ervin, an ORU professor, read some Scriptures and then he said, 'If you want to receive the Holy Spirit the Lord will give it to you . . .'

"Well, nobody had told me the baptism in the Holy Spirit was hard to receive, and I hadn't prayed more than 15 words until I was speaking in 'another language.' I had never been able to pray like this before. There was such a joy . . . such an inner release . . . all the bottled up frustrations of years began to melt away as I prayed.

"Just as soon as I left that prayer meeting, I called my wife and told her how I had received the baptism in the Holy Spirit, about speaking in tongues, and the wonderful release I felt inside. I also told her that I had made a Blessing-Pact and had given some Seed-Faith right then to seal it.

"Her immediate response was, 'You had better get on the next plane home—you sound like you are drunk.'"

A few months later Doris shared with me the rest of their miracle story. She said, "When Leo came home from the seminar he definitely was a changed man—and for the better! Every day when he left the house he would say, 'Today I am going to pray for the Lord to lead me to someone to whom I can witness.' And every evening when he came home I would ask, 'Did you get to witness to someone?'

"I'd never used words like these before. But I found in this that we were gradually growing back together. At least we were talking to each other.

"Leo started going to a little church but I wouldn't go. Nevertheless, he kept going. In fact, it seemed he just went to church all the time. Finally, on Mother's Day, he brought me some flowers. This was the first time he'd done anything like this in years. He had started giving to me first in such a warm and wonderful way, I couldn't keep up the cold war any longer, and right there in our home I gave my heart and my life to the Lord. Just a short time later I, too, received the baptism in the Holy Spirit. The prayer language I received really helped open me up. I now see that my so-called physical problems were spiritually-based. The Holy Spirit showed me how dependent I am upon God as my Source. There's a straightening out, a continuous opening up process going on in my life—and in our marriage.

"**In fact, the Holy Spirit turned our house into a home.** He first helped us with our marriage, then He bridged the gap between us and our children. Not only are we living and loving as a family, but we are also worshiping, working, and playing together. Life now has sparkle and meaning and we are constantly busy about God's business."

In this chapter you have seen a cross-section of marriage problems of real people just like you—people in various economic levels of life—high, low, medium—it really makes no difference. The fact seems to be that, regardless of your place in life, you either have a problem, you are a problem, or you live with one (as I've said many times). Also, I've wanted to show you the different ways that these people solved their marriage problems by putting the 3 KEYS of Seed-Faith to work in their own particular situation.

Most of them found that their BASIC problem was their lack of GIVING *FIRST*. I often say, "Show me a marriage that's falling apart and I'll show you two people who are trying to GET from each other instead of GIVING first." It's simple but it works.

The struggle is in coming to THE STARTING PLACE —IN CHRIST, where you are willing to give FIRST. But you can do it—just like these people did.

> If you will START looking and KEEP looking to God as your Source . . .
>> If you will START and KEEP seeding for a miracle, and then
>>> if you will START and KEEP expecting a miracle in your marriage,
>>>> IT WILL HAPPEN.

Boiled down to YOUR marriage—this means that you START WHERE YOU LEFT OFF. GO BACK IN YOUR MEMORY TO THE TIME YOU FELL IN LOVE AND LOOKED ON YOUR MATE AS A LOVING HUMAN BEING. Go out of your way to do the little deeds of thoughtfulness like you used to do. Don't attempt to establish who's to blame—right now that's not important. Regardless of who's to blame, YOUR PART IS:

> Key No. 1: Look to God as the Source of your Total Supply for a loving, forgiving spirit that you can't have without HIS help.
> Key No. 2: Seed for your Miracle by giving that

which is lacking (and you know what this is in your own situation better than anyone else).

Key No. 3: Expect your miracle—watch for it—it will come.

When you fall in love with Jesus and make Him the center and Source of your life, then it's possible to fall in love again with each other . . .and to build the kind of home that you both dreamed of in your days of courtship.

NOTES

13 HOW YOU CAN BECOME FAITH-CENTERED FOR MIRACLES IN YOUR FINANCES

IN 1970, Jack Shaw, a handsome young businessman, shook my hand and said, "Hi, Oral, how are you?"

"Fine, Jack," I replied. "I've just sent the manuscript of my new book, MIRACLE OF SEED-FAITH, to the printer. Believe me, it's a miracle to get all this out of me and into a form that can help someone else like it's helped me."

Jack said, "What did you say the title is?"

"MIRACLE OF SEED-FAITH."

"Man, do I need a miracle!"

I said, "Don't we all?"

"But I REALLY need one."

"What's the matter, Jack?"

"Well, first it's this tight-money market (remember, this was early 1970). I have houses finished, and no buyers. Also I'm 60 percent complete on a small shopping center I've struggled to get going. I started the center with a commitment from one of our local banks. The man said

197

when I was ready for the loan, it would be waiting. Now I've just been informed by the same man, NO MORE REAL ESTATE LOANS. I had really depended upon this source. Now it's cut off and I'm in trouble. I'm depressed. I just don't know what I'm going to do."

In Jack's face I could see the hurt, the bewilderment. He said, "I could lose . . . " and his voice trailed off.

"Jack," I said, "you remind me of what one of my associates said about me a few weeks ago, before I received a miracle that I needed from God."

Smiling wanly he asked, "What did he say about you, Oral?"

"Well, I had allowed this problem to get on top of me. In fact, I thought about the problem so much until I had become part of it instead of looking to God for the answer. I came in one day with this on my mind and my associate said:

> 'Oral, you look so low; if you died, they'd
> have to jack you up to bury you.'

"This really hit me. Here I was a man who believed— whose faith in God had brought him from nothing . . . and I was acting like an accident going off to happen."

Jack said, "What did you do?"

"Jack, I did the same thing I'm going to ask you to do. I asked myself, 'WHO IS MY SOURCE?' "

Jack looked puzzled. "What do you mean, who is my Source?"

"Just that. Who do you trust? Who is your Source? In other words:

> IT'S NOT *WHAT* BUT
> *WHO* IS YOUR SOURCE OF SUPPLY?"

As he was thinking that over, I dug into my briefcase and pulled out a typed copy of the manuscript of MIRACLE

OF SEED-FAITH. I said, "The book won't be off the press for 6 weeks, but take this typed copy, hole up in your room and read it. If you'll read it with an open and honest heart, you'll find some answers!"

He grabbed it like a drowning man. "I'll see you in the morning," he said.

Before I tell you what happened at daybreak the next day, I want to tell you more about Jack Shaw, of Greenville, South Carolina.

Jack is the son of Erby and Mittie Shaw, longtime friends of this ministry. Away back in the early fifties they had traveled to my crusades, seeking a deeper walk with Christ and asking prayer for some divine help for specific needs they had. Erby was building a little, selling extracts from door to door, and about anything else he could do to support his family.

Mittie and Erby Shaw, Jack's parents...

199

The living Christ whom I was preaching, and in whose name I prayed for the healing of people from every walk of life, came alive in Erby and Mittie as never before. Later they brought their children, among them Jack, a lad still in his teens.

As Erby absorbed the keys of FAITH and how to apply them to the everyday problems he faced, he saw how God wanted to bless and prosper him and his family. He taught this to Jack, and Jack soon launched out on his own in a small way in the building business.

Later Jack told me again and again, "I accepted Christ as a young boy. I love God. I want to make something of my life. I want to learn from you and others how to follow Christ and how to move forward in every area of my life, both spiritually and every other way."

Today if you drove through Greenville you would see signs before all kinds of new construction, "The house that Jack built." If you talked with people—in high places and low, in church and outside—they would tell you, "Here is a young man who's got it. He's going places."

Not that Jack is loud. On the contrary, Jack is quiet, serious, a hard worker, a devoted worker in his church, an active participant in his community, and, above all—according to his ability—a tremendous giver. One thing his parents learned through this ministry was to give and God would always multiply it back. This did not escape Jack's attention and soon he was giving, too. He saw that through giving, God opened up many things to him.

Jack ran for the South Carolina state legislature and won. Seemingly, everything he touched turned out right. He became the leading young builder in Greenville.

Then the tight-money market hit in 1970 and things fell off. It hit him just like it did everybody else. He had payrolls to meet, commitments made for new construction, houses, apartments, shopping centers, and new raw land and his resources were cut off.

People knew Jack as a dedicated Christian, and one who tried to reflect Christian principles in all of his business affairs. His word could be depended upon. But in this bad situation his last source of money to complete the project was cut off, and he was facing a dead end.

As he shared this with me, I realized that it was more than finances we were dealing with. Something deeper, more important, was at stake. Actually he was wondering:

If I fail, will those who know me as a Christian business-man wonder where Jack's God is?

I've given God credit for all my success; now with this facing me and not knowing where to turn, what's going to happen to me?

Have I the right to ask the Lord for His special help for this kind of situation or

Must I look to God only for the salvation of my soul and spiritual affairs?

201

I knew what Jack was feeling. The questions he was unconsciously asking had driven me away from God when I was only 17 years old, away from godly parents, the church, the Bible (on which I had been reared), and God himself. Even when I was carried back home too sick to live, really to die, I still couldn't relate God to the real situation I was in. When they surrounded my bedside those 5 terrible months, as I lay hovering between life and death, praying that my soul would be saved, I could not respond. God was a blurrr in my mind. I had pain. My lungs were bleeding. I needed a dose of life. They were talking about heaven; I was concerned about living here on earth.

Seven words from my sister Jewel helped me open my mind to God, to miracles. "Oral, God is going to heal you." All I had ever heard about God from a child up began to come alive to me when Jewel said those seven words to me. It exploded within me. God wants me to live. Me! Here! NOW!

My healing is another story, but with that I got on the right road and on that road miracles happened. Ups and downs? Yes. Obstacles? More than my share, it seemed. Failures, mistakes, even detours. But the road I got on was the right road. It led in the right direction. That road was not an "it"—it was a "Person," Jesus Christ of Nazareth, who became so REAL, so ALIVE to me and *in* me that it was almost like we were walking side by side in the flesh.

On this road I met the human race, people like me. People who hurt. People who had strayed. People who thought they had it all and had nothing. People—rich, poor; big, little; in the church, outside the church; educated, uneducated; workers, those on welfare; people who felt the joys

202

and sorrows of life in their "gut," people with needs—everyone with a need.

Somehow I began to learn how to get them on speaking terms with God, to make God real to them because He was to me. To get them together—giving, touching, reaching out. Together we got into the stream of miracles.

Facing Jack there that day on the ORU campus, seeing his downcast look, feeling what he was going through, I wanted to put my arms around him. I wanted to say, "Jack, you ARE a Christian; you know you are going to heaven. That's good. But

Jesus is so much MORE.

He's in the NOW!

He's at the point of this need in your life.

Because you have this need you can meet Jesus in a new dimension of understanding and trust."

Instead I said, "Read the manuscript of MIRACLE OF SEED-FAITH, and we'll talk in the morning."

It was about the middle of the next morning when I saw Jack again. He walked up to me with a spring in his steps, a lift to his shoulders, a light in his eyes. He looked excited and he was. In his quiet restrained voice he said, "Oral, I finished reading the manuscript at 6:00 this morning. I never did go to bed. I picked up the phone and dialed my wife Jane back in Greenville, and woke her up. At first she wondered if something had happened to me but I assured her it hadn't and that I was all right. I said, 'Jane, Honey, everything is OK now. Everything's going to work out.'

'Jack! what do you mean? What has happened?'

"I said, 'Honey, I found out who the Source of my Supply is.'

'You found out what?'

'I found out who my SOURCE is.' "

With eyes just gleaming Jack said, "Oral, I've been a Christian for several years. But early this morning

**I discovered for the first time in
my life that God is the Source of my
Total Supply as well as my Savior.**

I learned He is concerned about me as a human being with a wife and children, as a young builder, as a man with financial problems and all my human hang-ups. I no longer feel bad at my bankers or at the insurance people who have taken care of me up till now. They get their orders from the home office and had to cut me off, like they did everybody else, and left me high and dry. But you know, after learning they are not sources but instruments only I don't feel bad at them anymore. I'm going to look to God from now on . . . I will find the loans and everything else I need."

Tears filled my eyes. I knew Jack had needs—the biggest was this particular loan, and there were no visible prospects of one. Tight money would probably get tighter in the months ahead but I couldn't keep the tears of joy back. A change had come over Jack. It was so powerful you could feel the physical impact of it.

"Two things, Oral," he said, "I ask you to do."

"What are they?"

"First, let me take this manuscript home with me. I want Jane to read it. Then I want to read it every day along with my Bible. Second, there's a prime commercial piece of real estate at a choice location in our city. It's ready . . . I want you to pray with me . . . "

I said, "Jack! Last night you were worried over losing what you already had and owed for."

Jack and his lovely wife Jane

He smiled—really smiled. "Oral, that was last night. Today I know who my Source of Supply is. Better still, I know He controls many sources of financial supply I haven't thought of. I'm not going to worry myself by trying to find these new sources. I'm going to look to God my Source to open them up to me."

"Do you believe He will open them up to you?"

"Yes, Sir, I do." Then he said:

"There's one more thing I learned last night."

"What's that?"

"I learned that what I give is a seed I plant and that I can seed for a miracle by giving first and expect a miracle back from God my Source."

"Wait a minute, Jack. You've gotten deeper into the MIRACLE OF SEED-FAITH than I expected. You've always

205

given to the Lord. You and your folks have helped many people."

"Yes, we've tried. There's something we misapplied, however. Our giving has always been an obligation. We felt we owed it, that God has been good to us and we *should* give. But you showed me from Jesus himself that when we give first it will be given to us again. Well, I NEVER EXPECTED ANYTHING BACK. I have a check in my pocket I came intending to give, but I'm giving it with a different attitude now."

I said, "How do you mean?"

He said, "OK, you said in your book that our giving is not to be a 'debt we owe but a seed we sow.' I accept that. You said we were to 'expect the seed to be multiplied back in the form of our own needs.' That's a completely new thought to me but it's in the Bible and I accept it. Then you said to 'EXPECT A MIRACLE!' NOT FROM THE ONES WE GIVE TO OR HELP . . . BUT FROM OUR SOURCE, GOD. I've never done this before but I SEE GOD IN A WHOLE NEW LIGHT. HE IS REALLY MY COMPLETE SOURCE OF SUPPLY. I see that now for the first time in my life."

"Jack, my dear friend and brother," I said, "you were ready or you couldn't have grasped so quickly what it's taken me over 20 years to learn from the Bible. I tell you what God is going to do. You go home expectant, looking only to the Lord. Be confident and positive in this. Keep up Seed-Faith. You'll be surprised at the new ways of supply God will open. Sometimes it will be quick; other times very slow, but God will open them up, even in ways unexpected by you."

He nodded. I said, "Jack, through the seed you are putting into His great work, God will send you many, many miracles. He will multiply your seed sown. He will send the harvest, the miracle. So be sure and watch . . . be sure and be expecting a miracle. God will send it . . . but if you are not expecting it, you may not recognize it and it will pass you by. Then you'll wonder why God didn't help you when He was waiting for you to see it all the time. You see

> **When you put seed in**
> **and you really look to God your Source,**
> **there's no way the miracle won't come.**
> **Just be expecting it from Him."**

I would like to be able to tell you that when Jack got home—presto! Everything fell into place right off. But it didn't . . . it seldom does. To me, however, it makes it even more real when God our mighty Source does act.

Later I learned that FOR ABOUT 2 WEEKS JACK WAS PLAGUED WITH SELF-DOUBT. What he had read in MIRACLE OF SEED-FAITH, and all the positive things he had said to me in Tulsa, seemed to fade when he got back where the problems were—banks that still liked and believed in him but simply didn't have loan money available. Over a hundred men on the payroll, men who, with their families, had to eat.

Now picture this with me—here's Jack driving down the street. Two books are on the seat by him, his Bible and the typed copy of MIRACLE OF SEED-FAITH. He parks and reads, puts the manuscript down, picks up his Bible, checks the Scripture reference.

But my God shall supply all your need according to his riches in glory by Christ Jesus (Philippians 4:19).

Give, and it shall be given to you, good measure, pressed

down, shaken together and running over shall men give into your bosom. For with what measure you give, it shall be given to you again (Luke 6:38).

He that ministereth seed to the sower . . . multiplies your seed sown . . . (2 Corinthians 9:10).

If you have faith as a grain of mustard seed, ye shall say to this mountain, be thou removed, and it shall obey you (Matthew 17:20).

Therefore I say unto you, whatsoever things ye desire, when ye pray, believe that ye receive them and ye shall have them (Mark 11:24).

Beloved, I wish above all things that thou mayest prosper . . . (3 John 2).

Then he would go over the 3 KEYS in his mind.
Key No. 1: God is the Source of my Total Supply.
Key No. 2: Seed for your miracle.
Key No. 3: Expect a miracle.

It was in the Bible. It was good. But now he was alone with the same problems. Houses not selling . . . construction loans on them, with monthly payments amounting to thousands of dollars, with no money to continue payment unless the houses were sold. A BROKEN COMMITMENT FROM THE MAN AT THE BANK ON THE SHOPPING CENTER. Close associates with no idea of the struggle he was having.

Back in church Sunday morning. The choir sings great. The pastor's sermon is uplifting.

But Monday morning, the same old problems. "Sorry, Jack, our people say, NO MORE REAL ESTATE LOANS."

"But you said when my project was ready, to come back, I was covered . . ."

"Sorry, Jack . . . "

Pick up the Bible again—check the Scripture, the 3 KEYS. Read some more in the typed copy of MIRACLE OF SEED-FAITH about God my Source of Supply, and being at the point of my need.

HE'S MY SOURCE, but how am I going to come out of this?

That Oral Roberts, he got me stirred up. How did he build that university anyhow? He had nothing to start it with. I know, I was there. All that television time. Man, how? He says he found out who his Source is. I have, too. But how? How?

"Jane, Honey, how about our cash reserves?"

"What cash reserves?"

Yeah, that's right. In the construction business you don't keep cash reserves because you're always turning it back into building assets. So when your regular money sources dry up because of the tight-money crisis, it's time to get depressed.

My new shopping center is 60 percent complete. I am doing it on a commitment that the money will be here when I need it. But today my regular source for the money told me the home office had said:

"NO MORE COMMERCIAL LOANS"

The Bible says, "But my God shall supply . . ." It didn't say my banker would, or anybody else. It said GOD would.

I need to drive out into the country. Maybe I can think better. I've never doubted that God definitely directed me in the work I've undertaken. In fact, all my business deals are dealt with through prayer. I'm not talking about prayer down on my knees. I'm talking about the 'praying without ceasing' kind of prayer the Bible speaks of—the kind that as I go through the door of a place of business, or I'm

209

looking at a piece of property, I'm asking for special di-rection. I'm praying sort of like I'm breathing, just kind of naturally. It's just a part of me, the fact of God's partici-pation in all areas of my life.

As I say, I've never doubted God directed me in this work. But I've got houses on my hands that have sat for months. They WON'T sell. Houses just aren't selling. No one is selling houses.

"I picked up my Bible again and asked the Lord to just give me a word of faith. I knew God could speak to me out of the Bible but I never expected it out of Ezekiel—of all places!

"I've heard people say that they were reading the Bible and a certain Scripture just STOOD OUT ON THE PAGE to them. Well, this is really what happened to me—out of Ezekiel, believe it or not. I read in Ezekiel 36:26-36 and this is especially what spoke to me:

A new heart also will I give you . . . I will also cause you to dwell in the cities, and the wastes shall be builded. And the desolate land shall be tilled, whereas it lay desolate in the sight of all that passed by. And they shall say, This land that was desolate is become like the garden of Eden; and the waste and desolate and ruined cities are become fenced, and are inhabited. Then the heathen that are left round about you shall know that I the Lord build the ruined places, and plant that that was desolate: I the Lord have spoken it, and I will do it.

God had given me the gift of faith for this need and I never worried about these problems again."

A whole month passed. Jack and Jane went with some other builders to a home-builders convention in Texas.

"We were having a good time of fellowship but I was really uptight," Jack said. "Then all of a sudden what I

Jack, Jane, their twin boys Ronnie and Donnie, and little Deborah

had been trying to believe got down inside me . . . into my mind AND MY HEART. *I FELT CHARGED UP* with the fact that God was going to do something, and soon. I said, 'Jane, get packed, we're going home.' [This is like the 'flash of intuition' I mentioned earlier.]

"She could hardly believe me—this was only the first day of the convention. Nevertheless, we caught the next plane home and . . .

Within the next 6 weeks
we sold all those houses—
over three-fourths of a million dollars
worth of real estate!

This was a miracle. This was happening in our business, to the amazement of others. *But the greater miracle was that God overruled my desperation* to have been willing to sell

211

just to get back part of the money I had put up . . . and, in addition, gave us a fair profit! Then my faith really soared and I started expecting more miracles. I knew a lady that had a choice piece of land that adjoined a prime piece I already owned, and to develop it to its full potential I needed her acres. But not only I, but several other real estate men were trying to deal with her for it. She had already turned me down several times and other real estate men said, 'You'll never get it.' But soon after I returned home from the convention, she called me and said she was ready to deal! The amount I had to pay down was so small I almost had to pinch myself. She wanted me to have it. She said, 'Here, it's right for you to have it.'

"While I was recovering from that miracle, I received a call from an unexpected source for the loan I had been turned down on before.

"**Somebody big was moving in my life,** in my behalf. Somebody not boxed in by circumstances. Circumstances come and go *but He doesn't*. He's steady. He is THE Source.

"I could hardly believe it. And it literally astonished Jane. What with our twins and the new baby, she really hadn't got to read all of MIRACLE OF SEED-FAITH. But I'll say one thing, she never doubted that I was on the right track by making God our Source. And she wanted me to keep giving, even when the bottom was falling out . . . "

Nearly 3 years have passed since Jack made his great discovery. I could take up the rest of this book on at least ten other major miracles in his life and work. I'll tell only one.

Other builders and businessmen suffering the same fate as Jack, soon saw Jack was making it when no one else was.

They would look at him, then talk among themselves. Finally a couple of them dared to ask questions.

"HOW, JACK, HOW?"

Jack wrote for several copies of MIRACLE OF SEED-FAITH, now off the press. He gave them to ten of these men, saying, "Hole up somewhere with this book and your Bible; let God talk to you."

He said, "Oral, if I had bragged about how God was helping me, I might have turned them off. After all, I wasn't anyone special; yet if I hadn't been careful they would have thought so. I wanted them to discover for themselves who their Source is, and to learn that you receive through giving, that miracles do happen but only when we do what God has said in the Bible."

Well, these ten men included nine white and one black. The black man became deeply interested in the book, MIRACLE OF SEED-FAITH, that Jack had given him. Later he said to him, "Jack, I've been reading that book and watching Oral Roberts' television programs. And I've done some reevaluating in my own life. Just seeing what all this means in your life has had a great influence on me—if it can help you so much, it's bound to help me, too, if I look to God as the Source of my Supply, as the book says."

Each of the ten men read, studied, and absorbed the 3 KEYS. They began to move. There was no make-believe, no phoniness—just solid advancement where there had been virtually none. God became more real to them, to their wives and children, and associates.

One day I received a call.

"Oral, this is Jack."

"Hi, Jack, how are you?"

He laughed, "I still know who my Source is."

NOW HERE'S HOW TO CHECK YOURSELF WHEN IT SEEMS THAT SEEDING FOR A MIRACLE IN YOUR FINANCES ISN'T WORKING

Speaking personally, I was praying the other day about a problem that was beginning to get me down, when I remembered I must do something first for God before I asked Him for the solution to my problem. When I finished praying I took my Bible and I checked myself on the 3 KEYS by reading the Scriptures on which they are based.

I checked myself with Philippians 4:19, and asked, "Am I really looking to God as the Source of my Total Supply to solve this problem? Or am I just dwelling on the problem?"

Then turning to Luke 6:38 and 2 Corinthians 9:10, I asked, "Am I seeding for this need and expecting God to multiply back?"

Then I searched my heart and asked, "Am I expecting God to start giving me my miracle in the NOW for this problem?"

I have learned in problem after problem that asking myself these questions really helps. I find I can stop thinking so much about my problem and put my thoughts on God, who IS the Answer. God becomes bigger than the thing that is seriously affecting me. It also helps me to see that God has conditions for me to meet, and when I do I can rightfully expect a miracle, and sooner or later it will happen. I say sooner or later for God is going to act in His own way, and in His own time.

I want you to know that many of your problems can be answered if you check yourself on Seed-Faith first, and be sure you are sincerely trying to apply the 3 KEYS, always depending on the Lord and giving Him thanks every time He helps you.

This is why when I start a new project I practice giving something to the Lord first. Sometimes it's money, sometimes it's time or talent or extra concern. But each time, what I give represents my total being, my deepest love for God coming right out of my heart. Whenever I've done it in joy God has blessed me again and again. You know why? Because it's the scriptural way. It helps me make God my Source and to live expectantly for His miracles.

Another thing I try to do is to burn my bridges behind me and say:

"Lord, I'm going to take Your way; I'm going to follow You and give first and do it with all my heart, then I'm going to expect a miracle from Your hand . . . "

Jesus said, "Seek ye first the kingdom of God, and His righteousness; and all these things shall be added unto you" (Matthew 6:33).

You put God FIRST by making Him the Source of your Total Supply.

You put Him FIRST by seeding for a miracle—by giving something that represents your inner self.

Then you can EXPECT God to add the things you need for a successful life. I promise you MUCH, MUCH of it will happen in the now of your life on earth . . . long before you get to heaven. So much of what God promises is for you IN THE NOW of your needs and problems—for soul, mind, body, and circumstances—and the rest in heaven. He is Lord of all your life now and forever.

NOTES

14 HOW TO FIND THE MIRACLE TO OVERCOME YOUR FAILURES

AT THE BEGINNING of this ministry I had a soul-shaking experience with the fear of failure. Years before, the Lord had spoken deep inside me and said:

"Son, you are to take My healing power to your generation."

Then in 1947, He said:

"Now is the time."

In the days that followed, a nagging fear rose in my mind . . . it grew greater and greater until it almost overwhelmed me, threatening to stop me before I had even started. It was:

"What if I fail?"

It hit me like a bombshell. Finally I fell on my knees and prayed, "O God, what if I fail?"

And again, deep inside me, God said, "Son, you have already done that."

Then it struck me. What I had been doing was a failure. Now I had a chance to succeed if I could learn to really rely upon God, if I could truly make Him the Source of my Total Supply. I had no reason to be afraid of failure.

I had already failed;
now God was giving me the chance
to begin again.

I shall never forget the feeling of meekness that came over me. I had never felt so dependent upon God—or so SECURE.

I have learned since then that the fear of failure is responsible for more good things being left undone . . . more jobs not being asked for . . . more successful businesses never having been started . . . and more relationships never being restored . . . than any other factor.

So what do you do when you have failed? When things have collapsed around you . . . and you feel as if you are at the end of your life?

Jim Blanchett

I received a letter some time ago from Jim Blanchett, one of our partners who runs a construction business down South. In that letter was a $10 Seed-Faith offering. Later I learned that it was the Blanchetts' last $10 and their first step in Seed-Faith living. Sometime later, at a seminar on the ORU campus, he shared his story. He said:

"My business had gone to the bottom. To avoid bankruptcy and to keep my good reputation as an honest contractor, I sold all my equipment to the company I was building for and took a job with them as a foreman. I was left with a lot of debt and a salary that was just enough to take care of my wife and six children. **My job was a daily reminder that I had failed.**

"My wife Lucy and I have been Christians for many years, but I guess I really didn't know HOW to trust God as my Source in financial matters.

"Brother Roberts, when my business went under I started going downhill myself. I tried to go back into business for myself but I couldn't borrow money. I lost my self-confidence.

AND SINCE I HAD FAILED ONCE, THERE WAS THIS FEAR DEEP INSIDE THAT IT MIGHT HAPPEN AGAIN.

The constant frustration of not having enough money to make ends meet—and the feeling that I was locked in— was really getting to me. I'm sure I was hard to live with.

"**We felt we couldn't go on just 'getting by.'** We felt the answer was to go back in business for ourselves, even though this seemed impossible. We'd been listening regularly to your telecasts, Brother Roberts, and I heard you talking about looking to God as our Source, seeding for a miracle by giving first, and expecting a miracle. But we really didn't understand how it worked.

"Then Lucy said, 'Well, it worked for my sister [who is one of your partners]; maybe we should give it a try.'

"I argued, 'But we don't have anything to give—there's only $10 left in the bank!!!'

"And she said, 'I think we should give it anyway.'

"We both felt that the next step to receiving this miracle was to give to the Lord our last $10 as seed-money."

As Jim was talking I thought of the many people who

have shared with me how they felt when they took that first step toward receiving a miracle in the NOW of their need. Often it was a last desperate attempt . . . a feeling that "maybe, just maybe what Brother Roberts says about the 3 KEYS will work." And then after they had taken that first step, instead of feeling a great sense of faith and expectancy, some become afraid. I'm no different. Neither was Jim.

He continued, "Even when we had mailed our Seed-Faith offering the thought of having failed once kept nagging away at us, so we called the Prayer Tower in Tulsa and asked them to pray with us. As the prayer partners prayed we felt our faith rising and our fear lessening. We still had no idea HOW we could possibly go back into business but we knew we were looking to God as our Source, even for our finances. We FELT He would make a way.

"One day while at my job the general manager walked up to me and said, 'Jim, things aren't going like we want it to with our present contractor. How about your signing a contract and taking the job over again?'

"It happened so unexpectedly I heard myself saying, 'I don't have any money . . . no equipment . . . nothing. I can't do it!'

"He floored me by saying, 'I'll tell you what I'll do. If you'll sign a contract at your price, *I'll let you have all your equipment back at no cost. All you have to do is take care of the maintenance. Just keep up the equipment and it's yours.*'

IMAGINE A MIRACLE LIKE THAT!!!
It's just like the Bible says:

GOD IS ABLE TO DO EXCEEDING ABUN-
DANTLY ABOVE ALL THAT WE CAN ASK
OR *EVEN* THINK! (Ephesians 3:20).

So I was back in business again in the same place I had failed the year before."

But this was not the end of Jim's story. Remember, SEED-FAITH LIVING MUST BECOME A WAY OF LIFE, because when you get one problem solved there is always another . . . often an even *greater* challenge facing you. There is no so-called easy way. I sensed during that seminar that Jim and Lucy were burdened in spite of their victorious witness of how God had undertaken in their finances. I also knew that whatever the problem was, they were determined to find the answer. They came to me and said, "We want to plant some more Seed-Faith to help you with your television work and ORU."

Jim said, "When the Lord told me the figure I was to give, I began to argue, 'Lord, I don't HAVE that much to give,' and suggested a smaller figure. But I couldn't get any peace about anything less than the DEPTH God had told me. So we want to take this step into deeper faith."

During the prayer time, on the last morning of the seminar, as they came before me I said, "Jim and Lucy, you've had a lot of heartache . . . but God is your Source for this, as well as for your business. You've seeded for a miracle by giving first; now let's expect a miracle in this particular need you are facing today."

And we prayed together.

A year later they were back on campus again—and their faces were glowing. Referring to that time of prayer that we had together a year before in the seminar, they said:

"Right then we knew in our hearts that God had undertaken for our need. We had been deeply concerned about our son's spiritual condition—this was the need that we planted seed for at that seminar. And God has answered prayer!!! Today Steve is a wonderful witness for God and

221

is working with us in the business. We couldn't be happier.

"And another thing, Brother Roberts, after I got home from the seminar and began to go over my books, I was tempted to reduce my Seed-Faith giving. The devil began to remind me of all that I was giving already, the fact that I was just getting started in business again, etc. I realized right away that this wasn't the Lord. So I <u>doubled</u> the amount and told the devil to get behind me. And, believe me, that was the sweetest money I ever gave to God. (The hardest was when we gave our first $10.) And we weren't deprived of anything by this giving—nor was our local church, because we increased our giving to them as well.

WE LEARNED THAT GOD IS NOT GOING TO LET US GO WITHOUT A THING WE NEED IF WE PUT OUR TRUST IN HIM.

"**And, best of all, Seed-Faith giving has taken away the fear of failing.** Today we're building more than 200 houses a year and have 28 men on the payroll. Some weeks the bookkeeper will tell me, 'We're not going to make anything this week,' but at the end of the week there is always money to meet the payroll.

"**God has never let us down.** We just keep making God our Source; we just keep on giving Seed-Faith, and we just keep on expecting those miracles. And they keep coming. Our Christian work has grown more exciting and effective. When we talk about miracles happening in the NOW, we are talking from personal experience."

It's human to be fearful, to be afraid of failure . . . especially when we have failed. And most of us have. But the Bible says, "For God hath not given us the spirit of fear; but of power, and of love, and of a sound mind" (2

Timothy 1:7). <u>Fear of failure comes from wrong believing,</u> from the absence of faith in God our Source, as our personal Savior and as our Total Supply. When we really trust in God all the way, and in everything, we can know true security.

When we start becoming afraid, this is when we must start checking ourselves with the 3 KEYS. Am I really making God the Source of my Total Supply? Or is it my boss, or my business, or my paycheck? They are <u>not</u> your Source of Supply. They are only instruments. God controls the EXPECTED and the UNEXPECTED ways of supply because THE SOURCE is himself. If you lose your job and you look to God, in faith believing; if you seed for a miracle, then you can expect to RECEIVE a miracle. And it will come!!! But if you are not looking to God for a miracle, you may never recognize the miracle when He sends it your way. And you'll miss it. You'll wonder why the job doesn't appear—or if it does, why it isn't the right one.

I believe it is not only God's will that you have enough to get by on, but that you also prosper . . . that you succeed on your job or in your business or in your marriage or as a parent or as a student or in other ways important to you. And that your financial needs will be met abundantly!!

THE BIBLE SAYS, "BELOVED, I WISH
ABOVE ALL THINGS THAT THOU MAYEST
PROSPER AND BE IN HEALTH, EVEN AS
THY SOUL PROSPERETH" (3 John 2).

Make Seed-Faith living your way of life. Focus your faith on God your Source. Begin now seeding for a miracle . . . giving FIRST out of your want, your great need. This gives God something to work with. And EXPECT a miracle to happen . . . in the now of your need!

YOUR FUTURE IS AS BRIGHT AS YOUR SEED-FAITH!

THERE MAY BE LOSSES IN YOUR LIFE LIKE THESE . . .

AND LIKE THOSE JOB SUFFERED
IN THE BIBLE . . .

15 WHAT TO DO WHEN BAD THINGS KEEP HAPPENING

I WANT TO SHARE with you the story of some people who were like the man Job in the Old Testament. I want you to see Job and know him—above all, TO KNOW GOD AS HE DID. Then you'll see how these people overcame their troubles. I want to put Job's story in the NOW to give you a handle for your faith and to help you see how you can face your serious problems . . . for yourself . . . and for your family . . . and feel a knowing inside that you will receive your miracles. (Read the book of Job, especially the first three or four chapters, also the last chapter which is chapter 42.)

One day the devil said to God, "I don't like this man. I don't dig him."

God said, "Why not?"

"He's having it too good. He thinks all these things are coming from You. Take them away, give him some bad deals, let people turn against him, let him get sick and feel pain. Then You'll see he's not for real. He doesn't have an honest relationship with You, God. He's pretending to love You because of all the good things that are happening to him."

Ever wonder what the devil tells God about you and me? Does he tell God of our shortcomings and faults, our selfish-

225

ness and prejudices and fears? Does the devil put us in a bad light when he has a chance?

Well, it wasn't long until one bad thing after another started happening to Mr. Job. It came in like a flood. His children were in an accident. His business fell off and finally went under. He became ill in his body and couldn't work anymore. When he needed her the most, his wife misunderstood and walked out on him. Then his closest friends blamed him for what had happened to him and his family.

With his mind full of anguish and fear, his heart broken, with no one on earth to help him, Job wished he had never been born. He wished he were dead. Sound familiar?

ONE THING STANDS OUT IN JOB'S STORY. HE HELD ON TO HIS FAITH, AND TO THE FACT THAT GOD IS GOOD. AND THAT TOOK SOME DOING!

When people read the Bible they don't always see that God is a good God. They don't see these men and women as flesh and blood with serious problems and needs. They don't understand that what they did was to hold on to their faith and to continue to believe God is good. Although Job lost a lot, he clung to his faith in God. He discovered in a changing world the only reality, the only enduring thing, is faith in God.

Let's see how he clung to his faith and what the result was.

JOB'S SUFFERING

Everybody has a problem, or he is a problem, or he lives with one. This means everybody suffers at times—he suffers losses, is misunderstood, is forsaken, is all alone.

What's back of it? What causes it?

1. Job suffered as a result of what the devil did to him.

I believe there is a real devil. He's very real. He spoke

against Job and caused others to oppose him. It was because of the devil that Job was put through this very severe test.

2. Job suffered as a result of what men and circumstances did to him.

People were envious of Job. Accidents happened to his children and caused their death. It is what some people call the winds of chance, or being a victim of circumstances. The fact is, these things were beyond Job's control. There was nothing he could do to prevent them. He was struck, blow after blow, until he was utterly alone and helpless as far as man's power was concerned.

3. Job also suffered because of what he did to himself.

While viewing the collapse of everything dear to him, he said, "For the thing which I greatly feared is come upon me, and that which I was afraid of is come unto me" (Job 3:25).

THE THING I GREATLY FEARED . . . that which I was afraid of . . .

I know this language for I've faced fear all my life. And in every day's mail people say to me, "Oh, Brother Roberts, I'm so afraid such and such is going to happen."

Job put into words what he actually had done to himself. "I feared . . . I was afraid," he admitted.

To me, it's good to admit this. Get it out of your system. Confess it to God. Go on and say it, "God, I'm scared."

Job had believed the worst. He believed terrible things were going to happen—and they did. This is what constitutes fear, believing the wrong things instead of believing God!

To sum up Job's suffering, it was a combination of what

the devil and men and circumstances did to him, and what he did to himself by fearing.

WHERE ARE YOU TODAY?

Are you in Job's shoes? Wholly or partly? Do you feel deserted and alone? Is the devil really after you?

What about God? How do you feel toward Him?

Well, in spite of all you're going through, you can, through God's help, turn yourself toward God and trust Him as your Source. Don't sweat and fume because certain people and circumstances have let you down. They are not sources . . . but instruments only. As your Source of Total Supply, God controls the people and things He can use to deliver you out of all your troubles. Cling to your faith; don't give that up. It's the only reality you have left.

KNOW THAT BEHIND EVERY MIRACLE THERE IS A STRUGGLE OF FAITH.

For the Vanstones, it all began 5 years ago when the company Harry worked for merged with a national chain. The Vanstones felt Harry should resign, but with that resignation went a part of their lives and the security they had had for 14 years. He took another job but it just wasn't the same. Even church didn't have the same meaning that it had before—they soon realized that the entire family needed spiritual help.

About that time they began watching our telecasts and heard me speak about Seed-Faith—that God cares about us and will help us solve our problems. So the Vanstones became partners and started giving Seed-Faith regularly . . .

AND NOTHING HAPPENED!

In fact, things got worse!!! One day Mrs. Vanstone wrote to me and said:

Mr. and Mrs. Harry Vanstone

Dear Brother Roberts:

Things have gone from bad to worse. I have gone back to work to help with expenses--with two growing boys, you can imagine the grocery bills!!! Brother Roberts, our home used to be serene, now it's a mass of confusion. My youngest son is becoming so rebellious. His new sense of freedom,

229

*now that I'm not home all the time to supervise
his activities, doesn't help the situation. It's
just one thing after another...*

And that's the way it is in life—it seems you hardly get
one problem solved before another presents itself.

Well, the Vanstones continued to be faithful in seeding
for a miracle but it seemed that every time they gave, bad
things happened. For 3 years trouble was no stranger in
their home. They had a series of accidents, financial up-
heavals, disappointments, sickness, and more problems than
they had had in the previous 23 years of their marriage.
You name the problem—it seemed they had it. But in spite
of it all, Mrs. Vanstone's letter continues:

*During this time, I felt closer to my God
than at any period of my life. I found that He
is "that bridge over troubled waters." There is
nothing as insecure as the false securities we build
around our lives. God taught me many lessons.
Friends do, and will let you down--jobs do, and will
fail. GOD NEVER FAILS. We are quick to do God's
judging of others for Him, and look to sin and
sinner rather than person and problem. I also
found that God is a God of love, and will really
open the door if we want Him to come in. I thank
you, Brother Roberts, for helping me realize this.*

*Then it happened again. Due to a cutback in
jobs we were both out of work. I kept telling myself that things would work out. God has His purpose. When we gave seed-money it was money we
could have used for something else--or money we
couldn't afford--but then we knew that it was God
who was our Source and security. And through all*

of this we became very dependent on Him. We continued to seed for a miracle by giving. It tested our faith but we did it because we saw that this is what Jesus teaches.

This was about the time I called the Abundant Life Prayer Group and poured out my problem. And for 3 weeks after that call--another BLANK! NOTHING HAPPENED. Then suddenly our miracle happened! It was like a long pent-up flood breaking all around us. A job was offered to my husband far better than the one he had--better benefits, better pay, and 10 minutes from home. In our state, that is a miracle. I told him about calling my "Miracle Lady" in the Abundant Life Prayer Group and that she had told me to expect a miracle and to recognize it when it came. He was really thrilled. Then he told me he had been carrying your little plaque, SOMETHING GOOD IS GOING TO HAPPEN TO YOU, around with him all week.

We had often read the Bible together but when he asked me to read to him that particular evening, it meant something new and wonderful to both of us.

We still have our problems but to see them being solved, one by one, makes you know that Christ truly does care and when you seed for miracles, they will happen.

It is with humbleness and gratitude that we continue to practice Seed-Faith living--not in fear and frustration. You see, we don't expect one miracle--we expect a lifetime of them.

--Mrs. Harry Vanstone

231

You see, God may permit the devil to accuse you, and men and circumstances to make you suffer; but He always leaves some faith in your hearts. Faith is the one thing Satan cannot take from you. Many times the truth of this has saved my life, as it did Job's.

HERE'S WHAT JOB DID:

1. He clung to God his Source.

As he sat and suffered, he said, "Though God slay me yet shall I trust in Him. I shall trust my Source . . . My Source is God."

Consider that

> Job's trust in his wife and family did not *prevent* something bad happening to them.
>
> His trust in his associates and friends did not *prevent* their desertion.
>
> His trust in material possessions did not *prevent* them from being taken away, leaving him without money and with bills piling up. Therefore, he could not make any of these his source.
>
> Even the fact that he trusted in God did not make him immune to problems and suffering.

What it did do, however, was to give Job an anchor to hold to. BY TRUSTING IN GOD AS HIS SOURCE, JOB COULD HOLD HIMSELF STEADY WHILE EVERYTHING ELSE WAS SHAKING AROUND HIM.

Now the entire Bible teaches that God is the Source of your Total Supply. Everything and everybody else is an instrument only. THE BIBLE TEACHES THAT WHEN ALL ELSE FAILS, YOUR DIVINE SOURCE WILL NEVER LET YOU DOWN IF YOU TRUST IN HIM, IF YOU CLING TO HIM.

We should not be surprised that people change and fail

us, or that circumstances are sometimes against us. They are NOT our Source, and are not meant to be. We live on earth but OUR LIFE IS IN GOD. Our supply line is between Him and us, not between us and people and things.

Sometimes life can get mighty rough . . . AND UNLESS WE MAKE GOD OUR SOURCE IN LIFE'S TRAGEDIES, WE'RE NOT GOING TO MAKE IT. PUTTING OUR COMPLETE TRUST IN GOD AND HIS GOODNESS IS THE ONLY ANSWER.

I recently received a letter from one of our TV viewers who is living proof of this. She wrote:

Dear Brother Roberts:

I was divorced in June 1970. For 5 years I fought against the divorce and a nervous breakdown. Now, all I could think about was suicide. Even though I had been a Christian all my life, I felt far away from God. I prayed and begged Him to help me. I knew I had to live for the sake of my two children.

Then one Sunday evening in February 1971, after I put the children to bed, I was sitting alone feeling blue and lonely. When I switched on the TV, there was your Valentine Special. When you started talking about love, I sat up and listened. You said that God loves us, cares for us--that God is in the NOW.

I felt a kind of peace and contentment come over me that I'd been looking for. Afterwards I looked through the TV magazine and saw you had a regular half-hour show on Sunday mornings. So the following Sunday I hurried home from church and

watched it. I haven't missed a Sunday show or a
special since.

I sent for your book, <u>Miracle of Seed-Faith</u>.
It wasn't until December 1971 that I started to
practice Seed-Faith, but things began happening to
me in July. I worked in a small factory that had
financial problems and we went weeks without getting
paid. I used to get so upset I was sick and I'd
worry about the money and how to make ends meet
when he didn't pay us. I was also laid off a lot
of time. From <u>Miracle of Seed-Faith</u> I started
telling myself, "GOD IS MY SOURCE. HE SUPPLIES OUR
NEEDS AND I SHOULDN'T WORRY OVER IT." In July I
was paid most of my back pay and asked to work
steady again, and have been ever since.

Then in December 1971, I started using Key
No. 2: Seed for your miracle. "Give, and it
shall be given to you." Although I didn't have
much, I gave $2 to help in your great work for God.
I also gave Seed-Faith time. At Christmas time my
employer paid me up in full and gave me a bonus.
I knew this was from God so I gave my bonus money
as a Seed-Faith offering.

Right after Christmas I had a series of set-
backs. But I recognized it as God testing my
faith. Every day I said:
"SOMETHING GOOD IS GOING TO HAPPEN TO
ME TODAY. LORD, I EXPECT A MIRACLE."

And God has blessed me with extra time and the
money seemed to go further than ever. It's like
you described it. A happiness inside. Sometimes

*it's like a light shining inside me and I know
that at those times God is NOW, He is here beside
me. That He loves me and cares what happens to me.*

*Sometimes while listening to your telecast,
I feel so much love for God I cry. For the first
time in my life I have peace of mind. I can cope
with life and I'm expecting many more miracles.
My children also watch your program with me and
we hold hands while we pray. My daughter even
gets the Bible out and we use it as our point of
contact while praying. I know it is bringing us
closer together.*

**This letter was in two parts—the first section dated April
9; the second, April 17. The second section read:**

*As I finished writing the above testimony of
my faith, to my horror I discovered my 6-year-old
daughter had accidentally hanged herself in a tree
right outside my door. ONLY MY NEW-FOUND FAITH
AND TRUST IN GOD HAS HELPED ME GO ON. In my shock
and grief and sorrow, I asked God, why?*

I had faith.

I believed He loved me and my children.

I trusted God.

I was expecting miracles.

*It seemed that things were just beginning to
look brighter.*

*Why her tragic death right in my backyard,
almost right before my eyes?*

Why didn't I see her so I could save her?

Three people drove by and saw her but didn't

realize what had happened to her. Why did she have to die?

On Tuesday, April 11, as I was getting ready to go to the funeral home I was crying and talking to God, asking Him why. I thought, there must be a miracle in this somewhere. Then I felt God's presence; I felt my daughter's presence. She was with God. He had her hand in His and she said, "Hi, Mom. I'm in heaven and I'm so happy."

And God said, "The miracle is, you are born to go back to God, to be in heaven with Me. And that's where she is now--in heaven with Me."

I felt a happiness and peace inside of me and I didn't cry again until the next day at the cemetery. She bent down from heaven and gave me a last goodbye kiss.

I'm still lonely for her but I know she is very much alive in heaven with Jesus. ONLY MY STRONG FAITH AND TRUST IN GOD HELPS ME KEEP GOING. It keeps me believing that God does love me regardless of the tragic death of my beloved Jeweleen. I know and believe that God loves me and my son Martin, and as I continue to look to Him as my Source He will send me many miracles.

--Mrs. B. L.

2. Job finally put his faith to work by Seeding for a Miracle. He prayed for those who had hurt him. He forgave them.

To do this, Job had to start giving FIRST. Giving of his love and forgiveness toward others, and doing it first. (This is practicing Key No. 2.)

When Job had been successful and had money, he had given money to the Lord, to the widows and orphans, and to the helpless. Now he has no money left. But he has something he can give and he willingly gives it.

What did he have left to give? He had the ability to pray; he had the feeling for others. These he gave. The Bible says he "PRAYED FOR HIS FRIENDS" (Job 42:10). They were friends who had failed to understand him in his losses. They criticized and blamed him.

How he must have *wanted* to receive their prayers in his behalf. How he *needed* to receive. He could have demanded of God that he receive first. He could have said, "Someone pray for me first." Instead, he prayed for them. Sometimes it costs more to give forgiveness than it does money. It surely must have been hard for Job to pray for his friends first and forgive them. There is no record that they accepted his prayer or forgiveness. But they were not his Source. The important thing is what Job DID . . . as it is important to you what you do toward others.

You know God has placed faith, hope, and love in you. All these deeper and finer feelings are God-given. Your ability to pray, to hope, to love, to forgive, are gifts of God. They are real in your life. You've freely received; Jesus tells you to freely give . . . and give first (Matthew 10:8, Luke 6:38).

When Job gave his prayers and forgiveness he put in the seed for God to start multiplying all he had lost back to him. It was the seed he had put in that initiated a new positive action from God in his behalf.

3. Job got his miracle.

"And the Lord turned the captivity of Job, when he prayed for his friends . . . and [God] gave Job twice as much as he had before" (Job 42:10).

237

Through what the devil and people and circumstances had done to Job, plus what he had done to himself, he had lost everything. By clinging to God, his Source, by seeding for a miracle in opening himself up and giving forgiveness to those who hurt him, and doing it first, Job started expecting a miracle—his miracle—and he got not one but many!

God reversed the trend of what was happening against him. God multiplied back all he had lost—health, family, earnings, faith, love—giving him TWICE AS MUCH. He was twice as well off as before. This is the OVERFLOW Jesus talks about. "Give, and it shall be given unto you; GOOD MEASURE, PRESSED DOWN, AND SHAKEN TOGETHER, AND RUNNING OVER, SHALL MEN GIVE INTO YOUR BOSOM" (Luke 6:38). The giving to Job was overwhelming. It was when he needed it on this earth—in his lifetime—long before he went to heaven.

This is God supplying all your need ACCORDING TO HIS RICHES (Philippians 4:19). This is God causing the seed sown to multiply beyond what you can ask or think (2 Corinthians 9:10).

When you make God your Source, and Seed for a Miracle and Expect a Miracle and then ... sooner or later ... instead of a miracle, bad things start happening, remember:

1. In the midst of tragedy, hold on to your faith and to the fact that GOD IS GOOD. Discover in a changing world that the only reality, the only enduring thing, is your faith in God.

2. Behind every miracle there is a struggle of faith.

3. Job clung to God, the Source of his Supply. By trusting in God you can hold yourself steady while every-

thing else crumbles around you. The Bible teaches that when all else fails, your divine Source will NEVER let you down—if you trust in Him . . . if you cling to Him.

4. Only YOU can make God your Source. He loves you. He is nearer than your own breath. He is concerned and has all power to help you but only YOU CAN DECIDE if you want Him as your personal Savior and Lord. Only you can choose to make Him the Source of your Total Supply.

5. Job got his miracle. God multiplied back all he had lost—health, family, earnings, faith, love—giving him TWICE AS MUCH. This is the overflow Jesus talks about in Luke 6:38. And this is the kind of miracle that God wants to give you as you continue, in good times and bad, applying the 3 KEYS.

Keep expecting it.

Keep looking for it.

YOUR MIRACLE IS ON THE WAY!!!

NOTES

16

YOU HAVE SEEDED FOR MANY MIRACLES ... NOW IT'S TIME TO TELL THE DEVIL TO TAKE HIS HANDS OFF GOD'S PROPERTY!

FOR A QUARTER OF A CENTURY, this ministry has been one of daring faith. There have been times when I have had to TAKE THE RISK OF FAITH THAT HAS SHAKEN MY MINISTRY TO ITS VERY FOUNDATION. But God has never failed to prove His word. I'll admit there were times when I've been scared ...

when I've almost lost hope ...

when I couldn't see the way through ...

when I've made mistakes ... failed.

These times don't happen often, nor does the feeling stay long. But during these times my wife finds it hard to be near me. My men feel like avoiding me. Sometimes they say:

"You'd better steer clear of Oral—he's pretty low today ... "

Well, how do YOU react when your back is against the wall, and outwardly there's nothing going for you? It's terrible to lie down at night and stare into the blackness ... You hurt deep down inside the pit of your stomach. You drag out of bed in the morning—your eyes stinging from lack of sleep. Throughout the day you can't digest your food. You pace the floor. Your mind isn't on what you are doing. It's living hell when you lose hope—when you don't know the way out.

About 4 years ago God began speaking to my heart again about going back on national television. Inside, I was troubled. I'd been watching our nation forsaking God. I'd seen young people confused as they saw adults turning everywhere for help except to God. I'd heard people who went to church cry:

"WHERE IS THE GOD WHO IS RELEVANT TO MY NEEDS . . . NOW?" A whole new generation had come up not knowing God, spitting on the church, on the U. S. flag and government, and even on one another. They were truly sick inside—out of harmony with God and their real selves—which is often what sickness really is. I was reaching out for a way to reach the masses. And God began talking to me.

"GO INTO EVERY MAN'S WORLD."

"HOW?"

"THROUGH RELEVANT WEEKLY AND QUARTERLY TELEVISION PROGRAMS."

There was an excitement building within me as I began to see the possibilities.

By faith, I saw God meeting the needs of millions of people . . .

right where it's at . . .

in their homes . . .

through the medium of television.

On the other hand, I thought of the continuous struggle we would have with television stations to sell us time. I thought of the tremendous cost . . . plus, Oral Roberts University was still quite new and the financial load was unbelievable . . .

I thought of the possibility of failure (I've lived just

about everything you've read in this book) . . . the physical drain on me and the students to produce that many telecasts. There have been many times when I have been really scared to seed for a miracle, and this was one of them. IT WAS A RISK OF FAITH—A BIG RISK! At least that's the way it felt to me.

You can believe, I was shaking inside! Talk about mixed feelings.

I was excited!!! and—

I was also scared to death!!!

But the glorious thing about seeding for a miracle is that seed sowers have hope.

Now I was raised on a farm. I know it is hard work. You plow up the ground, plant the seed, cultivate the soil, and hoe out the weeds. And then you live in hope for the miracle of the harvest. SEED-PLANTERS—THOSE WHO GIVE OF THEMSELVES—HAVE HOPE. They are positive. People who do not plant seed have no hope. They are the "getters," tight-fisted, turned inward.

Planting seed is hard work—you sweat—you toil. . . and the ingathering sometimes seems slow . . . BUT, OH, THE JOY OF THE HARVEST! THE MIRACLES!!! GOD'S RESPONSE TO THE SEED-PLANTER'S HOPE.

It's like the little boy who said, "When I grow up I want to be a RETURNED missionary." In other words, he wanted to be able to tell the glowing stories of what God was doing on the mission field without being involved in any of the struggle on the nitty-gritty level of day-to-day life. We adults are not too much different. We'd like to be able to tell of triumphing over impossible obstacles and crises through the power of our faith in God, but not many of us want to go through the struggle of WORKING TO MAKE that miracle happen by putting the seed in first.

Well, we made the announcement to the staff that we planned to return to nationwide TV on an entirely new format, geared to meet the needs of the people NOW. Evelyn and I were looking to God and we decided together to seed for our miracle and to expect a return in the form of our need. And our immediate need was financing for the pilot program.

Shortly after this, a young minister came to us wanting to buy a piece of equipment that we no longer needed. It was an expensive piece of equipment. My immediate reaction was:

"PRAISE GOD!!!
HERE'S THE MONEY WE NEED
TO MAKE OUR FIRST TELEVISION
PROGRAM!!!"

But God said, and I heard the words deep inside me:

"NO, ORAL, I WANT YOU TO GIVE IT TO HIM."

You'd better believe the Lord and I had a long conversation over that one!!! It didn't make sense to GIVE this equipment away when we needed the money so desperately. And I knew what my men would think about it. I could almost hear them saying, "GIVE IT AWAY?"

So I argued with the Lord a bit.

"Lord, my men will have to agree because the equipment belongs to the Association."

Then the Lord seemed to say: *How about the Association doing a little seeding for a miracle?*

When I presented it to the men, they agreed. It was seed we sowed. AND IT COST US SOMETHING. It was given out of our want, our need. We saw that until there is some sacrifice, you have not truly given. You've merely given out of your surplus. (Remember this great truth back in chapter 4 of this book and in Mark 12:41-44.)

GIVE GOD YOUR BEST, THEN ASK HIM FOR HIS BEST.
THE GREATER THE SACRIFICE THE GREATER THE BLESSING.

"For with the same measure that ye mete [GIVE] withal it shall be measured [GIVEN] to you again" (Luke 6:38). (This is still part of Key No. 2.)

Many times partners have said to me, "I expected a miracle but it didn't come."

I say, "You didn't look LONG enough." The Bible also says, "Let us not be weary in well doing: for in due season we shall reap, if we faint not" (Galatians 6:9).

LET US NOT BE WEARY. Let us not grow *impatient* with our well doing, with our loving, our giving, our praying, our investing our lives in God's service. Let us not get impatient with that.

IN DUE SEASON WE SHALL REAP. You see, there's a *due season* in God. There is a due season for you if you plant some seed. In *due season* you shall reap, you shall have a harvest. It will come back, multiplied . . . again . . . and again . . . and again.

This Scripture hits me right in the face because I'm a NOW fellow. As one farmer said, "I want a hybrid harvest in incubator time." I knew what he meant for I want everything done yesterday. But I have discovered that God has His own timetables. God says, "If you don't get *discouraged*, if you *keep* looking to God for the miracle, you will get it." So what do you do when you don't get the miracle?

You *keep on* looking to God, the Source of your Total Supply.

You *keep on* seeding for a miracle.

You *keep on* believing

and expecting a miracle in the NOW . . .

245

You just *KEEP ON KEEPING ON*
until the miracle comes.
I've got at least a hundred miracles that are on the way,
that I have not received, for I have already seeded for them.
I get excited when I think about that. The Lord says:

"Now, Oral, if you won't get discouraged, if you won't
get weary—just keep seeding and keep on expecting the
miracle—you shall reap if you faint not, if you don't give
up."

WE SHALL REAP IN DUE SEASON

What does "in due season" mean? It's like going up to
a fruit tree—say it's an apple tree—if it's not due season
the apples will still be green and the only way you can get
one is to *pull* it. If you insist on picking the fruit before
it is ripe, you'll not be happy with the results. Any impatient youngster who has insisted on eating a *green* apple
can tell you that. But if it's the season and the apples are
ripened, you can touch the apple and it falls off in your
hand and it will be good. That's "due season."

WELL, THANK GOD! He took that piece of equipment
the Association gave as a seed we planted and multiplied
it over and over again in supplying finances for our first
tapings, PRIME TV TIME, and the many other expenses
involved in our television ministry. The harvest from that
seed-sowing is history now. What we are trying to do now
is to continue our Seed-Faith living. It's our hope God
will continue to multiply it back in the form of our constant needs as we make our witness to people who need
our Lord so much.

MARCH 1969 WAS

"THE SUBSTANCE OF THINGS HOPED FOR"
IN OUR RISK OF FAITH!

We're in your home each week on television with God's promise, "Something good is going to happen to you," through the gospel of our Lord Jesus Christ . . .

Richard and Patti and the World Action Singers from ORU joined me in reaching out to thousands of lives through the medium of television.

Our mail response broke all-time records. People wrote to tell us how God was working in their lives—

People from all walks of life!

247

Thousands of new people who'd never written before!

People from nearly every church background... and from no church background at all!

In their letters they shared their victories, their burdens, and asked for special prayer. In this, we personally began to experience a thrill in ministering as we stretched forth our hands to pray for people right there in their homes—we had never reached so many at one time before!

I just want to share a minute portion of the harvest we are reaping through our new television thrust:

Hopeless marriage restored

After 23 years of struggling with this seemingly hopeless marriage, my husband reached over and took my hand this morning while watching you on TV, and we prayed with you. I now have courage and reason to continue living with my husband...

--Mrs. H.T., Arizona

Delivered from alcoholism

I was an alcoholic for 35 years. I was so deep in sin I thought I had no chance. But when I began to watch you on TV and heard you say, 'God loves you no matter what you have done,' God spoke to my heart. That was 3 months ago and, thank God, today I know He has cleansed my body from it. I don't crave alcohol anymore, and I know Jesus is my Lord and Savior...

--R.L.H., North Carolina

Finds Christ; forgets suicide

My world seemed so empty. I had been ill, and I was lonely. I tried to commit suicide. Then I saw you and the World Action Singers on TV. I realized that the Jesus who made them so happy could help me, too. Now I thank God every day for the joy I found through Christ when I prayed with you that day. God became a Person to me through your ministry...

--A.M., Pennsylvania

Hostility replaced with God's love

My husband and I had decided to be divorced. We were sitting in hostile silence when your TV program came on. As you spoke we felt the warmth of God's concern for us, and we gave all our problems to Him. We're going to stay together because we believe the love of God will see us through.

--Mrs. P.R., Michigan

Saved and healed

My wife and I had drifted away from God. Even when we found out that I had a brain tumor, and later that it was malignant, we did not change our wild way of living. Then while watching your telecast, I came back to God. I could feel God's Spirit all through me, and the inoperable tumor was healed.

--C.W., California

Miracles in our relationship

Our whole family was in trouble. We couldn't relate to each other until we saw your program,

and through it we met Jesus. We have found God
in a personal way, and a closeness we didn't know
possible. We have taken Him as our Source, and
He has worked miracles in our relationships.

--The W. W. family,
Rhode Island

Remember, as you have read these testimonies, I've read them, too, and hundreds more that come in each month. It moves me deeply to see these people starting to put the 3 KEYS to work in their daily lives. You know as well as I do that life can get rough. It's here that you have needs—all kinds. When you get to heaven you won't have ANY NEEDS—OF ANY KIND. You'll be home at last— with God. But *right now* you are earthbound. It's like you're living in a "sea" of problems. The devil doesn't like you, or me.

I want to emphasize what I've been trying to share with you throughout this whole book. THE 3 KEYS ARE HANDLES. They are handles for your faith in God. They help you reach God, and God to do for you what He wants to do—give you miracle after miracle after miracle...

And now for something very personal. Since I finished writing this book, which I call THE MIRACLE BOOK, I am being challenged again. It's as if the devil says, "OK, Oral Roberts, I'll make you eat your words. I'll fight you on the 3 KEYS. I'll face you with new problems and needs. I'll hit you from every side. Then what will your friends and partners say?"

Well, all I can say to the devil is this:

"I've heard all that before. The Christ who lives in me has your number. On earth you struck at Him in His physical, visible form and 'bruised His heel' (humanity) but 'He bruised your head' (the very

250

center of your power) (Genesis 3:15). In His victory over death, through the Resurrection and ascension to God's right hand, He is the invisible, spiritual, unlimited Christ—fully invested with all His former riches, power, and glory. He has defeated you. I come against you, not in my own name or strength, but in His, and His alone. I charge you, Devil, in the name that is above every name, the name of Jesus Christ of Nazareth, TAKE YOUR HANDS OFF GOD'S PROPERTY!"

And I say to you, dear Friend and Partner, as I have gone back over THE MIRACLE BOOK again and again, I find I can't change a word, a line, a chapter. THE HOLY SPIRIT HAS ANOINTED ME TO BRING YOU THE 3 KEYS THAT ARE TOTALLY SCRIPTURAL! They are the same keys our Lord Jesus Christ used for miracles.

Remember . . .

GOD MADE MIRACLES FOR YOU—

AND YOU FOR MIRACLES!

I am praying for you to receive the biggest miracle of your life.

NOTES

ADDENDUM

THE 3 KEYS FOR MIRACLES MARCH ON IN VICTORY IN OTHER PEOPLE JUST LIKE YOURSELF...

Here are many more testimonies.
(Read them often.)

"WHEN I WAS IN PAIN I WOULD LAY YOUR LETTER ON MY CHEST AND THE PAIN WOULD SUBSIDE . . . "

WITH EIGHT KIDS and more bills than money, I had a lot to worry about. In addition, I had received a medical discharge from the army because of arthritis of the spine, and esophagitis. So I was out of a job and the slightest exertion would bring on a heart attack.

Then we began watching you on television. I knew God could heal. And I was beginning to understand and the more I listened to

Donald Carter

you preach, the more I began to feel deep down inside me that GOD WOULD HEAL ME!

Then one day I sat down and wrote you a letter. I told you about all my needs and asked you to pray for us.

Your letter back to me encouraged my faith, so I wrote again. Often in your letters you would say:

"This letter is anointed—
use it as a point of contact."

So when I was in pain I would lay your letter on my chest and pray, and the pain would subside. Somehow the anointing—or God's healing power—would come from God through your letters to me. With each telecast and each letter I would feel my faith growing.

Then one Sunday, all of a sudden, my neck just snapped. For the previous 6 months I had had to be in traction for a time each day to relieve the pressure and pain in my neck. But suddenly, in a moment, God healed me. The pain was gone!

The next day I had my neck X-rayed. The orthopedic surgeon came back with his report, obviously surprised, and he said, "There's nothing wrong with your neck."

Well, Brother Roberts, my physical problems were taken care of but I still had great financial needs. I had been hearing you talk about Seed-Faith, so I sat down and wrote you another letter. I told you of our great financial needs—that I needed a job and my daughter Elly wanted to go into nurses' training. This time I put in a seed-offering for the Lord, which I've continued to do every month since. And my way of thinking began to change—I began to expect a miracle! [Key No. 3]. It would take a miracle for Elly to go to school—for we didn't have the money.

A few days later I went to interview for a job and when I came home Elly was just bubbling over. She had been given a scholarship for her nursing education. A short time later I was notified that I had gotten the job—WITHIN A MONTH'S TIME Elly was in college and I was on a new job!! Praise the Lord.

To me, this is just more of my harvest from Seed-Faith giving [Key No. 2].

We've made God the Source of our Total Supply in our home. WHENEVER WE HAVE A NEED, WE SEED FOR A MIRACLE. Luke 6:38 is a proven Scripture around our house. We've learned to give in joy because it's always multiplied back manyfold.

Thank you, Brother Roberts, for your letters of encouragement, your telecast, and the concept of Seed-Faith living.

—*Donald Carter, Massachusetts*

"THANK YOU FOR CARING
WHEN OTHER PEOPLE HURT"

THE BOOK, MIRACLE OF SEED-FAITH, has helped crystalize my believing. When I received my copy, I read it and in my heart I said, Amen. All of the things Brother Roberts has taught for so many years seem to be compressed into this one book. I am applying the 3 KEYS of Seed-Faith to all the areas in my life that I've been passing up for years.

After I read MIRACLE OF SEED-FAITH I began writing to Brother Roberts regularly. That made a great deal of difference. I think that sometimes we don't realize what our needs are until we see them written out. I know it helps to write my needs down because when I do, I see them as they actually are—and it helps me see the steps I should take in putting the 3 KEYS to work for my needs.

Juanita Price

Writing this down also helps me to express needs to God, the Source of my Total Supply.

As I wrote of my need for deliverance from cigarettes, I began expecting a miracle [Key No. 3]. I turned my tobacco problem over to God. On January 16, 1970, I received my miracle! The desire for tobacco left me. I am still free and the desire for tobacco has been replaced with a desire to be close

256

to Jesus. I have been using the same Seed-Faith principles to get other needs met also.

My husband used to be rather sickly and could not work steadily. We committed that need to God and now he is stronger physically and spiritually.

Praise God for MIRACLE OF SEED-FAITH—and for you, Brother Roberts, and your dedicated staff—people who care when other people hurt.

—Juanita Price, California

"SALES HAVE TRIPLED"

WHEN WE FIRST LEARNED about MIRACLE OF SEED-FAITH you said to start using the 3 KEYS to get our needs met.

Rev. James Alexander

We had four children and a lot of bills. I decided to put God first in spite of our bills, and started seeding for a miracle in our finances.

I am an evangelist and also work part time as a salesman. I guess I could be called the least because I made the lowest. Within 4 weeks after applying the 3 KEYS to my life, my sales tripled until I was receiving $800 and $900 a week in commissions. In addition to paying my bills the Lord helped me make a large down-payment on a six-room brick home—the first home we'd ever owned. Also, I was able to get a luxury model car. I'm giving God more seed all the time to work with than I ever dreamed possible . . . and He's working with it. Praise God!

—Rev. James Alexander, Georgia

257

Mr. and Mrs. Ralph Lewis

"SEED-FAITH GIVING IS A WHOLE NEW WAY OF LIFE FOR US"

WHEN WE FIRST BECAME PARTNERS with Brother Roberts several years ago, my husband didn't even have a job. But we believe in Brother Roberts' ministry and felt the concept of Seed-Faith living made a lot of sense. But it was hard to get STARTED. We put in our seed-gifts for 3 months before we really found ourselves in the Bible spirit of giving, which is giving in joy. Then God broke through in our finances, and we've been able to give more and more . . . and always in joy. I feel that is the key, to be able to give with joy in your heart—and it goes along with what the Bible says, "The Lord loveth a cheerful giver" (2 Corinthians 9:7).

My husband is in the utility construction business, and right when other people weren't getting work God opened door after door for us. Now how do you explain that? We believe it is Seed-Faith. It's trusting in God and expecting miracles from Him. He's the best SOURCE we've ever had.

—Mr. and Mrs. Ralph Lewis, Florida

NEW JOB AS
GENERAL MANAGER

THE COMPANY I WAS WORKING FOR was going under financially and so were we. About the time things looked the darkest, we learned about Seed-Faith living through applying the 3 KEYS. We had always trusted God for our lives in a vague sort of way. But Key No. 1—looking to God as

Mr. and Mrs. Harold J. Decker

259

the Source of our Total Supply—was rather new to us.

So we tried Key No. 2—seeding for a miracle by giving —and BANG! While we were on Key No. 3, the miracle happened. It didn't take long for us to see what God could do. Right out of the clear blue sky another company asked me to come to work at a higher salary. Three months later I was offered another job as general manager at almost double the original salary. There has been an overflow from unexpected sources to meet our needs, and then some.

—*Mr. and Mrs. Harold J. Decker, California*

"YOUNG PEOPLE CAN ENJOY THE BLESSINGS OF GOD, TOO"

BROTHER ROBERTS, young people can enjoy the blessings of God, too. Since I learned about the 3 KEYS of Seed-Faith

Boyd Carson

living, I immediately put them to work in my life. I started looking to God as my Source and putting Him first in my life, and He has blessed me with a good car, a large check from an unexpected source, a good raise, a better position in my company, a Sunday school class to teach, and the assurance of my needs being met in the future.

I call all of these my Seed-Faith miracles—a result of seeding for miracles in every area of my life [Key No. 2].

—*Boyd Carson, Indiana*

260

"GOD GAVE US A TRIPLE-HEADER"

I AM WRITING to tell you how God has given us a triple-header miracle and He did it all in one week's time! I am so grateful to Him I want to go on record by this letter so that you can share our joy and relief, since it is through concerted prayer and the application of the teachings of the 3 KEYS of Seed-Faith living that you keep drumming away at to all of us who would listen. Over a period of time I've been studying it, and then one day I could say in my heart, "I believe it!" I finally accepted the fact that God really cared about us and wanted to do good things for us. Then I considered your next point, "God is the Source of our Total Supply" and I studied that a while, over a period of months, and I decided you were right—that was true, too.

Eleanor McCutchen

The giving part of the 3 KEYS you teach was the next thing that really turned me on. I've never, in all my experience, had it explained so well. It always puzzled me before you spelled it out by comparing Old Testament times with New Testament, and I saw where we fit into the picture today. It makes you feel real good to KNOW how to be a Christian and be SURE you are pleasing God by giving gladly, much less finding the key to the supply line from heaven! This is what you must mean by giving in joy. And I've found it to be a real thrill to give in other ways than money, too. Now we talk about this at home and we enjoy each other more when we understand this concept of seed-giving. ALL the giving means something, not just to whoever gets—but to God, too. He wants us to know this! Thanks a million for getting it across. I'm now a willing fan of yours. Helping support your work means much more to me now.

And now the miracles: All three of my sons have got new jobs—all in one week, after waiting for months! First my son-in-law Eric, who had been doing odd jobs for about 6 months, got a steady job and the odd jobs poured in so fast he had to line them up to take care of them all. Then my son Rick, who was on a part-time job, too, since graduation, got a job full time, and starts today. And finally, through him his brother Bob, who was not working at all, started last week on a new job. The whole atmosphere in our family has suddenly changed. It's a miracle. A triple-header!

We were fresh out of money, we gave, and now our needs are being met; it works. Praise God and thanks for your prayers.

—*Mrs. Eleanor McCutchen, Oklahoma*

"I COULDN'T JUST SIT AROUND AND SEE OUR NEEDS OVERWHELM US"

I WAS INTRIGUED by what Oral Roberts said on his telecast about seed-giving and I sent for his book, MIRACLE OF SEED-FAITH. As a child of God, I knew I had to do something. I couldn't just sit around and see our needs overwhelm us. The company that my husband works for had already discontinued one shift, and further cutbacks were planned. He was concerned that the layoff would hit him next. My daughter was in college and expenses were high. We had built a new home but it flooded so badly at every rainfall that we had to move back to our old home. The old place needed redecorating. We were going to do it by buying the materials as we could and doing the work ourselves. But we were short of funds all the time. It seemed if we made two steps forward we went three steps back.

Then I read the book. And I put the 3 KEYS to work.

Cornelia Rice

After I started seeding for our miracles, I told my daughter to count on getting the teaching job she was training for, to constantly picture herself in a classroom, teaching. (I didn't even realize that suggesting this visual prayer was saying, "Expect a miracle") [Key No. 3]. And I kept praying about my husband's job, and giving in faith.

Then things began to happen. First, I noticed the seed coming back in the form of our need. My husband was asked to work extra hours. A few months before, he'd had to demand his share of overtime. My daughter got a teaching job. She signed the contract months in advance. I know that practicing the principles of Seed-Faith got her the job. It is nearly impossible to get a teaching position in our area.

By the end of the year my husband was working so many hours that we didn't have time to work on remodeling our home. So I began to plant seed-time. I began to give time to the underprivileged youth who work in the government agency where I am supervisor. On my lunch and coffee breaks I tried to help them with their personal problems. Soon, my husband and I found time to begin work again on our home. We were able to finish it by the time our daughter came home for the holidays.

We have done more in our home in this one year than in the 3 previous years put together. We overcame our financial problems, even with one daughter in high school and another graduating from college. And I know that Seed-Faith has been the reason for my husband's job being so steady. When I started my seeding for a miracle it was hard to find money to give, but now I know the answer is to give first, in everything. Then God multiplies back what we give—whether it's money, or time, or whatever our needs are. It works.

—*Mrs. Cornelia Rice, Ohio*

"YOUR LETTER SAID:
'BE WATCHFUL, GOD WILL BE AT WORK . . .' "

MY BUSINESS, a small retail grocery store in a textile neighborhood, was in desperate need of a financial shot in the arm. I had extended my credit to the limit. I knew without even approaching a bank for additional money that my assets were insufficient to use as collateral.

I wrote to you, Brother Roberts, and requested prayer for my life—spiritually, physically, but economically, mostly. You answered me back in a wonderful letter of faith. You pointed out the 3 KEYS. I had already recognized God as the Source of my Total Supply and I had put in seed—but the last thing you said in the letter was, "Be watchful, God will be at work." This was Key No. 3— Expect a miracle! And I started watching. During these

John Thaxton

last few weeks since that time, God has manifested himself in a wonderful way.

Cash sales in the first 2 weeks alone increased by 57%. It had to be a miracle. I hadn't advertised in the local paper or on the radio. I hadn't been on top of the building shouting about all the good things inside. But God had touched me at the point of my need.

By the end of these 3 months the cash intake, when compared to the second quarter of the year, had increased by 76%.

In between the time of my first Seed-Faith gift and prayer request, I had increased the offering twice and entered into a Blessing-Pact covenant with God. I was giving God more to work with. My gifts for God's work have been multiplied back to me in a most beautiful way.

Your ministry has given me an insight into Christianity and an awareness of God and His Son Jesus Christ that I never knew was possible. When you say on the TV program, "Something good is going to happen to you," I believe it!

—*John Thaxton, Virginia*

"I LOOK FORWARD TO EACH NEW DAY WITH REAL JOY!"

SINCE I LEARNED ABOUT SEED-FAITH LIVING I have started to put the 3 KEYS to work in my everyday life. God has helped me to witness for Him in a wonderful and greater

Charlie Kidd

way. I am also glad that I have learned that even witnessing for Him is seed that I plant that can be multiplied back to me in the form of my need. And, already, God has multiplied my giving and witnessing back 'to me in the form of my need [Key No. 2].

Shortly before Christmas I had an attack of emphysema so bad that my doctor was going to put me in the hospital. I had to gasp for every breath. But my wife Grace called the Abundant Life Prayer Group; they prayed for me and I was healed. Praise God!

I have my own little drive-in cafe. Where I once was bedfast, I now work 15 to 16 hours a day and I've never felt better. What a day it was when I learned that God is the Source of my Total Supply and I know I can expect a new miracle every day [Key No. 3].

Thank you, Brother Roberts, for pointing me to Seed-Faith living. Now I look forward to each new day with real joy.   *—Charlie Kidd, South Carolina*

"I Came To ORU Without The Full Finances For Even One Year . . . THANK YOU FOR THE CONCEPT OF SEED-FAITH LIVING—IT REALLY WORKS!"

THANK YOU for my 3 years here at ORU. Thank you for the 3 KEYS of Seed-Faith living. They work. Each year I have come back to ORU without the full amount for tuition, board, and room. But the Lord has supplied my need, as I looked to Him as the Source of my Total Supply, so

Lydia Mathre

that at the end of the semester my bill could be stamped "Paid In Full."

God put me at ORU for a specific purpose. It wasn't by accident. I have had many opportunities to minister and to learn. Praise the Lord!

Thank you, Brother Roberts, for letting the Lord use you as His special instrument . . . your dream—ORU—is a reality. God has touched my life and the lives of many other students through your ministry.

—Lydia Mathre, California

267

"SEVEN LITTLE REASONS
WHY I KNOW
SEED-FAITH WORKS"

I MUST SHARE WITH YOU an exciting discovery I have made.
When Brother Roberts pointed out the 3 KEYS in his book,
MIRACLE OF SEED-FAITH, I tried very hard to understand.
You see, we have seven children. When I had to take all
seven to the shoe store I often found I didn't have enough
money to go 'round; some of the children had to wear shoes
that still pinched their feet. For several years when this
happened, or when they needed clothes and I couldn't clothe
them properly, I would ask God to make the company who
employed my husband raise our salary. Until recently, I
had expected everything to come out of my husband's check

from that company. I've learned now that God is the Source of our Total Supply and that He can supply in many ways, even from unexpected sources [Key No. 1]. Well, this helped me to start looking to Him more. I was able to redirect my thinking toward God as Source. And it works! For instance, not long ago my husband attended a convention for accountants. There, he learned of a government accounting institute at a certain university that fit right into his doctoral program. Not only was he able to go, but he was paid for going. The money he was paid took care of our debts plus one thing we had not counted on—our washing machine went out and we were able to replace it also.

Now, when we have a need we know it will be met because we live the Seed-Faith way. We always give God something to work with and because God is our Supply and we look to Him for our "NOW" needs—such as buying shoes or clothes for our children—we don't have to wait. God is our Source and we get the shoes or clothing now!

So, you see, we have seven reasons why we know Seed-Faith works. This concept has become a way of life. And what a wonderful way it is.

—*Mrs. Robert Feller, Oklahoma*

"I was skeptical at first, then . . .
SEED-FAITH TRUTHS FINALLY SANK IN"

BROTHER ROBERTS SENT ME a copy of MIRACLE OF SEED-FAITH. As I read the first principle of Seed-Faith—looking to God as my Source—I said, "Now come on, let's level. Maybe 20 centuries ago, but certainly not today. Maybe this worked with a guy like Abraham, who was an itinerate kind of fellow, moving around a lot and living in the fields —maybe even for Moses—but certainly not today."

I had a lot of walls to climb over and barriers to pull down. Because I was suddenly thrust from "God is dead" to God is alive and knowable.

Matt Fliss

But when the concept finally sank in, it caught me. I felt a real vitality in this truth.

As I studied MIRACLE OF SEED-FAITH, I saw that it was in giving that you receive [Key No. 2]. The whole idea of Seed-Faith seemed so natural, being based on sowing and reaping, times and seasons. I sensed it was for real and my skepticism melted away.

As I practiced the 3 KEYS of Seed-Faith living consistently, I saw it working in different areas of my life. I was never a person who could save money. But when I started giving consistently I found that not only were my own personal needs met, but I was also accumulating savings. Then I found that giving included more than giving money.

I am an adjunct professor of community service in one of the colleges in our city. And in this capacity I saw many new opportunities to give of my knowledge, service, friendship, time, and talent.

I am also the assistant director of Upward Bound (a government program for underprivileged high-school students similar to Head Start for underprivileged preschool children). I find real joy in sharing material means, understanding, counsel, leadership, friendship, and guidance with these teen-agers.

Outside my regular work I find extra time to give, working with the migrants in our area. Just recently we have received a federal grant that has enabled us to help these people with their material needs. I give credit to the Lord.

The Lord has made my work a joy and a blessing. Instead of changing my situation, He has changed me. He has opened my eyes to the love and beauty in my friends, students, and colleagues. Also, He helps me to serve as an instrument in helping to meet others' needs.

Through all this, He is fulfilling my dreams. I'm turned on by God and He's tuned me in to His frequency.

I'm finding that problems are really only challenges. As quickly as a problem begins, a solution seems to pop up.

I now understand that certain things work in your life, if they are scripturally based, regardless of man-made theories (and I have studied many ideologies and theories). I personally know that Seed-Faith works! Through learning and practicing this concept of giving in joy and expecting God to meet the needs in every area of my life, I have found joy, love, and peace.

—*Matt Fliss, Pennsylvania*

"IT'S A DREAM COME TRUE"

TWO YEARS AGO we had very little to be happy about. We had only enough money to feed our family of seven for 2

weeks. When that ran out we didn't know what we would do. We were living in a cramped city apartment and the rent would soon be due. Then one morning we turned on the TV and heard you say that God is in the NOW and that God is concerned about ALL our needs. You outlined the 3 KEYS of Seed-Faith. I had attended church all my life but had never heard anything like this. But it made sense, and I felt that I should put in some seed even though you didn't ask for anything from us. Really, we didn't have the money to give—we gave out of our want! And we began to EXPECT a miracle!!! [Key No. 3].

One week later my husband got a very good job that he had tried to get twice before. We also received an unexpected financial present. We gave part of this as more seed and continued to seed for miracles regularly [Key No. 2]. During the year we received many other blessings.

And each time our seed is multiplied back, we give God more seed to work with.

Now we are buying our first home!—in the country with lots of room for the children to play. It's a dream come true. My husband has received two promotions in the past year. Our future is very bright.

I thank God every day for what He has done and for what He will do. Without God, we had nothing. And I thank God for your regular telecasts which showed me how to bring His abundance into our lives.

—*Mrs. Brenda Conley, Massachusetts*

"I DIRECTED MY NEEDS TO JESUS AND BEGAN TO EXPECT HIS MIRACLE FOR ME"

I WANT TO SHARE WITH YOU a miracle that is still taking place. God is so wonderful and loving! He has honored every gift and multiplied every seed I've planted in faith.

My miracle concerns being accepted into college. When I was a junior in high school I planned to come to ORU, but my father died before I graduated and I felt it wouldn't

Irene Patros

be right to leave my mother alone with my two small sisters, so I put off going so far away to school.

In the meantime, Mother had read MIRACLE OF SEED-FAITH and begun to give Seed-Faith money in each of our names. I took over my own Seed-Faith pledge and all through my last year of high school, I paid it myself. I di-

273

rected my need to Jesus and began to expect Him to show me His way [Keys Nos. 1 and 2]. I prayed and I gave. Always somehow I'd get the money to keep my pledge, sometimes through the instrument of a baby-sitting job, sometimes in other ways, but always the Lord supplies it.

Jesus guided me to apply to a fine college in my town. I did, but I was not accepted at first. Then Mother wrote you and requested you to pray that God would make a way for me to attend college. Just a few weeks later the miracle that I'd been expecting came! I was admitted to the college in my town. Not only that, but I was given a scholarship which will pay my expenses for all 4 years! Without my heavenly Father's help, I could not have this. How thankful I am to know that God is the Source of my Total Supply!

Now I am in college, and I know that although the Lord used many people as instruments, He was the only One who gave me this miracle. Jesus is alive in the NOW of my life. I love Him very much. He has literally multiplied and blessed my small seed thousands of times.

—*Miss Irene Patros, New York*

"IN DESPERATION, WE BEGAN OUR ADVENTURE IN SEED-FAITH LIVING"

WE NEVER COULD HAVE PLANNED all the miracles that have happened since we called the Abundant Life Prayer Group to ask for prayer about my husband's job situation. It was pretty bad. He was working long hours and sick half of the time. We felt that there must be a better job for him somewhere. We wanted to have some time to work for God, too. We had read MIRACLE OF SEED-FAITH, but until our situation became desperate we really hadn't tried putting the 3 KEYS to work. So after we called for prayer we felt we should do the next step and seed for our miracle. Our gift truly represented our whole hearts, for we were at the point of desperation.

In just 2 months a job opened up for my husband as a computer programmer for a medical center in the Midwest. I have sisters living in that city but I had

The Matthew Tierneys

lived in California for 15 years. It is a miracle that the Lord has worked—not only the job, but for me to be with my sisters again. And God saw to it that we found used furniture that we could afford, even just the right piano that I wanted so badly. It's almost too much to put into words what God has done for us since we planted our seed of faith. Now, we're glad that we reached the point of desperation because that is when we called the Abundant Life Prayer Group and began our adventure in Seed-Faith living.

—The Matthew Tierneys, Missouri

Something **GOOD** is going to happen to you

EXPECT A MIRACLE

These faith-building plaques are yours free without obligation — write and request yours today

Also my book,
MIRACLE OF SEED FAITH,
is free on request and without obligation.

313

NOTES

NOTES

NOTES